The Edible Woman

MARGARET ATWOOD'S

The Edible Woman

A Reader's Guide by W. J. Keith

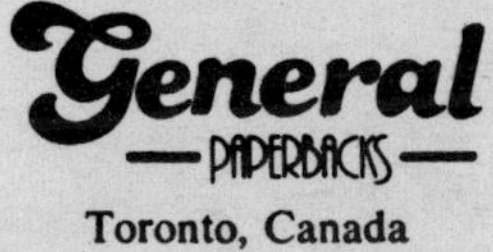

Toronto, Canada

Canadian Fiction Studies No. 3

Published in hardcover by ECW PRESS in 1989

General Paperbacks edition published in 1990

ISBN 0-7736-7248-6

The cover features a reproduction of the dust-wrapper from the first edition of *The Edible Woman*, courtesy of the Thomas Fisher Rare Book Library, University of Toronto. Photograph of Margaret Atwood by Graeme Gibson © 1989, reproduced courtesy of the photographer.

Printed in the U.S.A.

Table of Contents

A NOTE ABOUT THE AUTHOR

W.J. Keith was born in England and graduated from Cambridge before immigrating to Canada in 1958 to pursue graduate studies at the University of Toronto. After gaining his Ph.D. in 1961, he taught for five years at McMaster University before returning to the University of Toronto, where he is now Professor of English at University College. Before turning his full attention to Canadian literary studies, he established himself as an authority on the rural literature of England. His publications in Canadian literature include *Charles G.D. Roberts* (1969), *Epic Fiction: The Art of Rudy Wiebe* (1981), and *Canadian Literature in English* (1985). *A Sense of Style: Studies in the Art of Fiction in English-Speaking Canada* (including a chapter on Atwood) (1989). He has also edited *Charles G.D. Roberts: Selected Poetry and Critical Prose* (1974), *A Voice in the Land: Essays by and about Rudy Wiebe* (1981), and (with B.-Z. Shek) *The Arts in Canada: The Last Fifty Years* (1980). He was editor of the *University of Toronto Quarterly* between 1976 and 1985 and was elected Fellow of the Royal Society of Canada in 1979.

NOTE ON EDITIONS AND REFERENCES

The text of *The Edible Woman* used in this commentary is the New Canadian Library edition, first issued by McClelland and Stewart, with an introduction by Alan Dawe, in 1973. Page references to this edition are given in parenthesis after each quotation; this pagination is virtually identical with that of the three 1969 editions published in Toronto, London, and Boston, and with the Virago edition published in London in 1980.

The Edible Woman

Chronology

1939 Margaret Atwood born 18 November in Ottawa, the second of three children (an elder brother, Harold, had been born in 1937).

1940-61 Spends most summers in Quebec and Ontario bush country, where her entomologist father conducts research.

1945-46 Family moves briefly to Sault Ste Marie.

1946 Family settles in Toronto, where father teaches at University of Toronto.

1951 Younger sister, Ruth, born.

1952-57 Studies at Leaside High School, Toronto; contributes prose and verse to school literary magazine.

1957-61 Studies in the Honours English program at Victoria College, University of Toronto, where she is taught by critic Northrop Frye and poet Jay Macpherson. Discovers Canadian literature. Contributes poems and prose to college magazines, including

	reviews of Margaret Avison, George Johnston, and James Reaney (reprinted in *Second Words*), and satirical articles cowritten with Dennis Lee.
1961	First book publication, a privately printed chapbook of poetry, *Double Persephone*, wins E.J. Pratt medal. Wins Woodrow Wilson Fellowship on graduation.
1961-62	Becomes graduate student in English at Radcliffe College, Harvard University. Gains her M.A.
1962-63	Begins Ph.D. studies at Harvard; meets James Polk, American fellow-student and writer.
1963-64	Works briefly for a market-research company in Toronto. Conceives the idea for *The Edible Woman*.
1964-65	Teaches English at University of British Columbia, where she writes the first draft of *The Edible Woman*.
1965-67	Continues doctoral studies at Harvard, planning dissertation on "The English Metaphysical Romance" with special emphasis on H. Rider Haggard.
1966	*The Circle Game* (poetry).
1967	Wins Governor General's Award for *The Circle Game*. Marries James Polk.
1967-68	Teaches English at Sir George Williams University [now part of Concordia

	University] in Montreal. Revises *The Edible Woman* for publication.
1968	*The Animals in That Country* (poetry).
1969	*The Edible Woman* published in Canada, England, and the United States.
1969-70	Teaches creative writing at University of Alberta.
1970	*The Journals of Susanna Moodie* and *Procedures for Underground* (both poetry).
1971	*Power Politics* (poetry). Begins to serve on board of House of Anansi Press.
1971-72	Teaches English at York University.
1972	*Surfacing* (novel); *Survival: A Thematic Guide to Canadian Literature*.
1972-73	Writer in Residence at University of Toronto.
1973	Divorce from James Polk; moves to Alliston, Ontario, with Canadian novelist and interviewer Graeme Gibson. Awarded, by Trent University, the first of her many honorary degrees.
1974	*You Are Happy* (poetry).
1976	*Lady Oracle* (novel); *Selected Poems*. Daughter, Jess, born.
1977	*Dancing Girls* (short stories), *Days of the Rebels: 1815–1840* (history). Gains City of Toronto Book Award and Canadian Booksellers' Association Award for *Lady Oracle*.

1978	*Two-Headed Poems* (poetry); *Up in the Tree* (children's literature). Visits Australia for Writers' Week.
1979	*Life before Man* (novel).
1980	*Anna's Pet* (children's literature). Moves with Graeme Gibson and Jess to Toronto.
1981	*True Stories* (poetry); *Bodily Harm* (novel).
1982	*Second Words: Selected Critical Prose.* Edits *The New Oxford Book of Canadian Verse in English.*
1982-83	President of Writers Union of Canada.
1983	*Murder in the Dark* (short fictions and prose poems); *Bluebeard's Egg* (short stories).
1984	*Interlunar* (poetry).
1985	*The Handmaid's Tale* (novel).
1986	*Selected Poems II*. Edits *The Oxford Book of Canadian Short Stories in English.*
1987	*The CanLit Foodbook.* Elected Fellow of the Royal Society of Canada.
1988	*Cat's Eye* (novel).

The Importance of the Work

The editors and publishers of the present series have asked me to begin my discussion of *The Edible Woman* with a section of between eight hundred and twelve hundred words under this general heading, explaining why Atwood's book deserves the attention of contemporary readers. The request troubles me because I can express all that I consider necessary to say on the subject in just five words: it is a good novel. Yet something more is obviously required. In the case of a novel like *The Edible Woman*, moreover, the problem is compounded. It is not only a good novel but a good comic novel, and to write at length about the importance of the comic is to risk pomposity.

Why should a novel be read? Why should the reading of a novel be considered "important"? There are all sorts of possible answers to these questions — most of them dubious. Canadian nationalists, for instance, are likely to argue that the novel should be read because it is Canadian, but country of origin is a bad reason in itself (even if it can be called a reason at all). Of course — I hope I am justified in writing "of course" — Canadians should be well read in the literature of their own country, but why should this particular novel be read? There are large numbers of bad Canadian books, just as there are large numbers of bad books written in most countries, and there is no compelling reason why we should waste our time with them. *The Edible Woman*, I repeat, merits attention not because it is a Canadian novel but because it is a good one.

Nonliterary reasons for reading novels, or literature of any kind, are always suspect. They are numerous, and nationalism is only one of them. In the current climate of opinion, it is common to urge the claims of a novel like *The Edible Woman* for feminist or, more generally, for political reasons. I shall be considering these approaches in the next section, but the point that needs to be made here is that, however significant the subject of a novel may be, the ultimate test will be its quality as a work of literary art. It is possible (and quite common) to encounter a very bad novel that deals with a very important subject, yet, if the artistic quality is poor, the standard of commentary and insight will almost certainly be low. A novel is important, then, not because it concerns itself with an important subject but because it is well written.

Why (once again) should a novel be read? In a society that places a heavy emphasis on practicality and usefulness, the question is loaded, since one cannot make the only reply that would be accepted without question — that the act of reading adds to the Gross National Product. This is in no sense a flippant or irresponsible statement. On the contrary, it indicates in a paradoxical way why *The Edible Woman* is profoundly important: because the novel forcefully, dramatically, and even radically challenges the priorities by which "importance" is measured in our society.

But this, someone may wish to object, is surely a "nonliterary" reason? Not really. Artists — and this is as true of painters, sculptors, and musicians as of poets, dramatists, and writers of fiction — perform a valuable function in society because, through their art, they provide us with alternative ways of looking at the world and at ourselves. Sometimes they can help us to find interest or beauty or significance in the ordinary objects around us that we might otherwise take for granted. Robert Browning, the English Victorian poet, writing a dramatic monologue in which the speaker is the Italian Renaissance painter Fra Lippo Lippi, puts the following words into his mouth:

> . . . we're made so that we love
> First when we see them painted, things we have passed
> Perhaps a hundred times nor cared to see.[1]

Sometimes, artists challenge our ideas about what is possible by inventing new worlds startlingly different from our own, whether Shakespeare's magic island in *The Tempest* or an unknown planet in the latest science-fiction fantasy. Sometimes again (and here *The Edible Woman* fits in), artists can produce a portrait of our society that disturbs us because it makes us realize that aspects of it which we have accepted as natural or inevitable or "normal" (to use a recurrent and essential word in the novel) may in fact be recognized as unnatural, challengeable, and abnormal. Such a work (if sufficiently well written) can be "important" in jolting us out of our lazy and inert assumptions.

Margaret Atwood wrote *The Edible Woman* about Toronto in the 1960s; I am writing about her book while living in Toronto in the late 1980s. As we shall see, her portrayal is not "realistic" in a photographic, documentary sense; she selects certain aspects of the life she knew, exaggerates some, plays down others, and ends with a novel that offers, through comedy and satire, a disturbing view of the ways by which a particular society moulds the lives, attitudes, and options of the people who live within it. Since the society in question is governed by the basic principles of what, for want of a comprehensive term, we may call our Western-urban-capitalist-industrialized-materialist democracy, there will be few readers who will not feel that Atwood's radical shafts come close to home. Whether one lives in a larger metropolis than Toronto, or in a small city or smaller town, outside Canada or outside North America, or even if one lives in the country, one will have been influenced in some way or another by the kinds of societal norm portrayed here. This, you may say, is a "political" statement, but it is political in the broadest sense. *The Edible Woman* is not urging you to vote for one political party rather than another in the next election; it is not advocating a specific course of political action that could be outlined in a white paper. It is political in the one way in which an artist may legitimately be political: by showing rather than telling, by exposing the politics of social arrangements in terms of how they affect human beings. Because it is a witty and probing and well-written and well-crafted novel, it helps its readers to think and feel, to respond imaginatively to the conditions of the world they inhabit. This is not by any means the only role that art can play in society, but it is a significant and honourable one.

A literary-critical axiom, extending back at least as far as Roman times, states that the artist's function is to teach and to delight. *The Edible Woman* delights because of its sharp wit and the changes it rings on traditional comic situations (an aspect to be considered in detail later). The solemn-minded, of course, always assume that teaching is more important than delighting, a view that can lead to heavy dollops of unassimilated didacticism. On the other hand, the kind of entertainment that is revealingly called a pastime — something that passes the time or "kills" time — soon palls. If we are sensible, we hope to learn something while we are being entertained, whether that something is about ourselves or about the world around us. The artist's ideal, then, would seem to be to teach in the very process of delighting. *The Edible Woman* does just that. It is a good novel because it is well written; because it is well written it can expand our imaginative awareness; and because it expands our imaginative awareness it may be considered "important."

(Much to my surprise, in this section I have now written rather more than twelve hundred words.)

Critical Reception

Whoever starts reading a book will eventually end by expressing a judgement of some sort.[2] The kinds of reaction can vary drastically. One may be excited, bored, amused, puzzled, involved, detached, infuriated, impressed, shocked, moved, etc., etc. Sooner or later, however, one will be impelled to come to some more definite kind of evaluation: "I like this book," or "I can't see why others consider it so important." Such judgements are inevitably personal, which is why many people are reluctant to make them; who am I, they ask, to declare that this is good or bad? But we soon come to realize that, whether we want to or not, we are required to make such judgements continually, and that consequcnces follow from them. Shall I go to see this film, or rent this video? Shall I watch this television program or another on a different channel? Is this a book I merely borrow from a library or should I buy it? And it soon becomes clear that the more important of these decisions depend upon such factors as moral maturity or emotional growth. On some matters, it is a positive duty to have carefully considered opinions. To dismiss questions of taste as trivial or arbitrary is a mistake, partly because the fact that they *are* acutely personal is itself of extreme importance. As the English critic F.R. Leavis wrote: "My critical judgment is mine, in the sense that I can't take over anyone else's (if I did, it would cease to be a judgment)."[3]

This observation seems to me profoundly true, but it raises some inevitable questions: If I don't take over anyone else's literary judgement, why read literary criticism? Why discuss (as this section proposes to discuss) what other people have written about *The Edible Woman*? Why, for that matter, read the present book, in which I am shortly to offer my own literary-critical approach to the novel? There are a number of legitimate answers to these questions. First of all, different readers bring different expertise to bear upon a book, different knowledge that may well prove useful. A writer with a sound background in psychology, for example, may well be able to offer insights into the motivations of characters in the novel that would not occur to the average reader. Someone who has made a special study of the history of comedy or the development of satire may respond to subtle effects that others would miss. Because I happen to be a few years older than Margaret Atwood and can remember Toronto in the years in which she wrote about it, I may be equipped to say something of interest about the book that would be beyond the scope of anyone whose memory goes back no further than, say, the mid-to-late 1970s. But more important than specialized knowledge is the simple fact that, when a work of literary complexity is involved, one person will recognize effects that another fails to notice, and vice versa. Literary criticism, when informed and of high quality, is a collaborative venture; it can enrich an individual's reading of a given text because it brings together the shared responses of numbers of skilled readers.

All this is leading up to a simple but very significant point. In the next few paragraphs, I shall be describing and evaluating a number of different discussions of this novel. I shall then proceed to offer my own commentary. These sections can be helpful to readers if — and only if — they have already read the novel attentively and have come to some personal conclusions about it. They will then be in a position to test their own responses against those of others. But there is no point in consulting other discussions unless *The Edible Woman* has been read and pondered first; otherwise, if the criticism is read first and the novel afterwards, readers will merely notice what they have been alerted to notice. The same applies to the detailed "reading" of the novel presented later in this book. It is *not* intended to provide reach-me-down opinions that can be taken over without question or qualification; if it were, it would merely be functioning as part of the producer-consumer syndrome that is Atwood's chief satiric target in her novel. A book like *The Edible Woman* deserves to be read carefully and critically, and so does any literary comment upon it. Some of the earlier discussions of the book I find myself quarrelling with, and I shall attempt to counter them since it would be improper in this section to sit on the academic fence, refusing to take sides. To gain any benefit from the rest of the book, readers must be prepared to weigh my judgements on the novel, and on the previous criticism that has been devoted to it, in order to decide for themselves which seem persuasive and satisfying and which do not. Once they have gone through this process, modifying their own responses in some instances, fortifying them in others, thoughtfully accepting or rejecting what is presented here, their own personal judgements will have developed to the point where they are informed, considered, and (because alternatives have either been assimilated or countered) essentially their own.

It is usual, when surveying earlier critical judgements on a novel, to begin with the original reviews. In this case, however, little is to be gained from such an approach. The standard of literary reviewing in Canada has generally been poor, and for the most part the reviews of *The Edible Woman* reveal a depressing incapacity to read the novel on its own terms. Robin Skelton, for instance, in the *Malahat Review* complained that Duncan "is quite unbelievable" (108) without seeming to question whether credibility on a realistic level is a necessary criterion (are Prospero and Caliban in Shakespeare's *The Tempest* "credible"? Is Superman or Snoopy?). He also complained about "the total absence of any tenderness in the relationship between the various lovers" (108) — which is rather like insisting that there are very few laughs in *King Lear* (true but irrelevant). Anne Montagnes, in *Saturday Night*, called it "superficial" (56), an adjective that seems to me to apply to the review but not to the novel. Gordon R. Elliott, in the *West Coast Review*, fell back on cliché. Reviewing both *The Edible Woman* and Margaret Laurence's *A Bird in the House*, he wrote: "In two new Canadian novels, . . . young people find an identity" (68), which means precisely nothing. He also classified Atwood's novel as a "brief to the Royal Commission on the Status of Women" and as "a 'university' book" (68). Do such reviewers actually read the books about which they pass judgement? One of the few reviews of *The Edible Woman* that can be recommended is George Woodcock's in *Canadian Literature*, which accurately described the book, compared it intelligently (in terms of both style and content) with Atwood's poetry, and shrewdly praised "the extremely capable way in which Miss Atwood has handled the element of fantasy which has become a key element in the New Fiction" (99). Otherwise, with the exception of Tom Marshall in *Quarry*, who found the whole novel "delightfully, wickedly funny" (55) and wrote perceptively on Duncan, the reviews tend to vary from the blandly or solemnly condescending to the lamentably inaccurate.

A systematic reading of the discussions in books and critical articles soon identifies two common weaknesses that inhibit anything approaching a full response to the novel's special qualities. One of these (just alluded to) is the tendency to treat the novel too solemnly (not "too seriously" but "too solemnly"), laying insufficient emphasis on the comic effects within it. The second (related) weakness is to approach it not for itself but for evidence that can be assembled for a nonliterary purpose (generally political, sociological, feminist, or psychological).

These two basic weaknesses are both illustrated in what, I fear, is a classic instance of how *not* to read *The Edible Woman*, Elizabeth Brady's "Towards a Happier History: Women and Domination." This article was written specially for a politically oriented volume entitled *Domination* (commissioned by the University League for Social Reform). Brady's is the feminist contribution. It consists of three sections, of which the third — "The Twentieth Century:

'Oh, Screw My Femininity' " — is devoted almost exclusively to Atwood's book. The critic is not, however, interested in the novel as a novel, but only as a source of ammunition for her sociopolitical, nonliterary thesis. She focuses relentlessly on the exploitative work at Seymour Surveys and elsewhere as part of "the larger domination structure of consumer capitalism"; Peter, for example, simply "represents a strong social norm that is buttressed by the group" (30). Brady's general procedure is summed up in the following passage:

> Atwood's analysis of woman's predicament has been executed on several levels: each of the different female roles is examined — woman as underpaid worker divorced from production; as lover/mistress alienated from her emotions; and as mother/wife whose capacity for maternity subverts everything that falls outside of her reproductive function. . . . (30)

The trouble here is not that Brady says anything that can be proven untrue, but that her selection of material and the crude rhetoric into which she translates it lead to a shocking distortion of Atwood's creative achievement. Who would realize, from the passage just quoted, that a sparkling comedy containing highly amusing scenes was being described? Brady's account, when checked against the text, proves to be deceptive. Marian has a healthily sceptical attitude towards Seymour Surveys, but she does *not* see herself as an "underpaid worker divorced from production." Clara may be preoccupied with "her reproductive function" in an early chapter of the novel, but Atwood makes Marian describe her as looking "like a boa-constrictor that has swallowed a watermelon" (31)! Here the difference in tone is essential. The point is that Atwood naturally thinks as a novelist while Brady automatically views everything in terms of political radicalism. She even quotes a speech by Duncan — a character who, as we shall see, is constantly making misleading and disorienting statements to force Marian out of her passivity — as if it were a straightforward not-to-be-qualified political statement on the part of Atwood. It would, of course, be folly to deny that *The Edible Woman* has political implications, but to reduce the book to a piece of political propaganda is a grotesque falsification. Few interpretations of the novel are quite as blatant as this, but too many of them err in this direction; they *use* the novel for their own purpose and ignore whatever fails to fit. Ironically, the result is often a crass vulgarity at least as bogus as the society that Atwood satirizes in her own infinitely more perceptive way.

Because *The Edible Woman* first appeared in 1969, a period of sociopolitical unrest in most parts of the world, a period when feminism was becoming an increasingly important topic, and also a period when a sense of Canadian nationalism was at its height, these are the "nonliterary" approaches that might be expected to be particularly prominent. In fact, the nationalistic approach is fairly muted, mainly because Atwood does not offer a convenient handle for such an emphasis within the book (her next novel, *Surfacing*, with its stress on Canadian/American relations, provided a more obvious focus for this kind of thematic study). The more general sociopolitical approach is more appropriate here and receives acceptably accurate and legitimate treatments in Sheila Page's "Supermarket Survival" and Alan Dawe's New Canadian Library introduction.

A feminist emphasis is more problematic. Atwood herself, in various interviews as well as in her later introduction to *The Edible Woman*, has noted that the book was written before the movement got conspicuously under way, but that it was published "just in time to coincide with the rise of feminism in North America" (*Second Words* 370). I shall be touching on this subject at various points in the course of my commentary. Here it is sufficient to state that, because the novel is written by a woman, and has a woman protagonist who finds herself at odds with her society, an important element in the book is clearly conducive to feminist treatment. But *The Edible Woman* is a novel and not a tract; to read it as some kind of feminist propaganda will inevitably lead to a serious distortion not only of Atwood's intention but of the text itself. Her target is broader than feminism; Duncan and even Peter — though he never gets to the stage of realizing it — are just as threatened by the predominating values as Marian, and the fact that Atwood provides her protagonist with a male (albeit idiosyncratic) guide-cum-guru is sufficient proof that her position cannot be confined within the limits of the feminist cause. Besides, the extremes of feminism are themselves parodied by Atwood within the novel, as we shall see. Feminist readings, like all other nonliterary readings, can illuminate the text so long as they remain faithful to both the content and its tone; but too often they distort the novel by extracting a simplified didactic "message" and neglect its artistic subtlety.

Some scholarly articles begin with what seems to be a nonliterary approach, but nonetheless, because they bring special knowledge to the text, succeed in deepening our literary appreciation. One example is "Femininity, or Parody of Autonomy," Elspeth Cameron's gathering together of all the medical information about anorexia nervosa, the technical name for the condition which afflicts Marian in the novel. This provides useful background for readers unacquainted with the subject, though its application to the novel is limited by the fact that most medical research on anorexia postdates the novel. Cameron's report therefore provides some stimulating analogues to the presentation of Marian, but not sources for Atwood; for this reason, the paragraphs in which she applies her findings to the book are less convincing, and the later parts of the article need to be read with caution. Similarly, T.D. MacLulich's "Atwood's Adult Fairy Tale" brings some interesting anthropological and psychological perspectives to bear on the novel. In this case, however, I consider the writer especially liable to the temptation of pushing his arguments too far. At one point, for instance, so eager is he to fit Marian's story into his thesis that he refers to her "aversion to sex" (124), for which there is no evidence (think of the bathtub scene [59–63]!); Marian certainly develops reservations about a particular marriage, but that is a very different matter. Elsewhere, MacLulich argues against the text that, because Marian's cake-woman is smaller than herself, it really represents a child. If this were Atwood's point, she would have made it clear (or, alternatively, is open to criticism for not so doing). MacLulich, at his best a shrewd critic, has here gone astray because he tries to fit—or force—*The Edible Woman* into his chosen pattern instead of following the text and letting Atwood's meanings reveal themselves in their own way.

For the most part, it is safe to assume that the most useful critical discussions of the novel (and this is generally true for all fiction, indeed for all literature) are those which start from a more strictly literary approach to the text. As its title suggests, Catherine McLay's "The Dark Voyage: *The Edible Woman* as Romance" is a case in point. Briefly, McLay is struck by the tension within the book between the surface-plot (will Marian marry Peter or not?) and the deeper psychological patterns of ascent and descent that seem to characterize the book. She identifies the latter as the patterns of literary romance and provides an interpretation of the book consonant with this argument. The approach is not, however, without its dangers. Frank Davey in his book-length study has specifically named this article, along with two others on *Surfacing*, as examples of interpretations that in his view "confuse the characters' fictions with the author's fiction, mistake novels which deconstruct archetypes for novels which confirm them" (67). The point is both well taken and crisply expressed, a convenient instance of thoughtful and challenging criticism, though I don't believe that it seriously undermines McLay's argument. It seems to me that Atwood's novel steers a skillful middle course between deconstructing archetypes and confirming them. Patterns of ascent and descent are constant in Atwood's work, in her poetry as much as in her fiction. Davey is right to insist on the parodic element in Atwood's tone in much of the novel (McLay, like most commentators, veers towards the side of the excessively solemn), but wrong to suppose that Marian's experience is not to be regarded as a version (comic, to be sure) of a representative pattern in human life. McLay's argument, like most others, is open to argument and qualification, but it provides a basically intelligent, sensitive, and accurate commentary on the text.

Much the same can be said of Robert Lecker's "Janus through the Looking Glass." Lecker is looking for points of comparison as well as contrast between Atwood's first three novels, *The Edible Woman*, *Surfacing*, and *Lady Oracle*. He is especially interested in the "circular structure of the narrative" (177) in all three books, the way in which all three protagonists are left at the end of their respective novels in a still equivocal position, with their options barely clearer than they were at the beginning. Lecker is careful to distinguish the very different tones of the three books but nonetheless sees them as variations on a similar theme or pattern. He lays particular emphasis on their ambiguities (". . . Marian MacAlpin's story is triumphant *because* it is ambiguous . . ." [178]), and he is especially stimulating in this challenge to the either-or dichotomy (victor or victim, producer or consumer, success or failure) that so much criticism — and, to some extent, Atwood herself with her "double Persephones" — seems to encourage. Lecker's article is provocatively sceptical of standard readings, and, although one need not necessarily agree with him, no one can read his article without receiving an enhanced impression of the novel's complexity.

Other literary approaches can be considered more briefly. Linda Hutcheon, in "Atwood and Laurence," contrasts this novel with Margaret Laurence's *The Stone Angel* and explains certain differences by reference to Atwood's previous experience as a poet. The argument is, I think, a little oversimplified in its emphasis, but it serves a useful purpose in directing our attention to what she calls Atwood's "solid scaffolding of imagery" (258). "Even the narrative technique of the novel," she argues later, "becomes subject to the imagery" (259). This is criticism, all too rare in Canadian commentary, that insists on verbal elements as central to the meaning and effect of a literary work, and is especially welcome for that reason. Jayne Patterson, in "The Taming of Externals," takes a linguistic approach by upholding an interpretation through detailed analysis of the linguistic niceties of selected passages. The results do not, in my view, justify the erudition and its accompanying jargon (the main points she makes reveal themselves clearly enough in any careful reading), and some of her literary conclusions seem to me dubious to say the least. But at least the emphasis is where it should be — on the subtleties of language.

Jerome H. Rosenberg's inevitably brief treatment in his introductory book *Margaret Atwood* is accurate, workmanlike, unexceptional, but more coherent and far better written than Sherrill Grace's equivalent section in *Violent Duality*. Perry Nodelman (who, like Grace, misspells Marian's first name throughout) argues in "Trusting the Untrustworthy" that ". . . Atwood intends Fischer's discussion [of *Alice's Adventures in Wonderland* in chapter 22] as a guide to the workings of Marion's [*sic*] subconscious . . ." (76); this is, on the face of it, doubtful since Nodelman is taking a passage which in the novel is clearly presented as parody and is offering it here as if it were an unequivocal model. I am not denying that aspects of Fish's performance cast some light on Marian's dilemma (if they did not, the justification for the passage's existence might well be in question); I would insist, however, that they cannot be extracted without distortion from the comic context to which they belong. Nodelman, surely, has paid insufficient attention to the tonal clues provided by Atwood within the novel.

John Lauber's "Alice in Consumer-Land," despite his continual misspelling of Marian's surname, settles down after an uncertain start to become a stimulating, often original (though poorly edited) reading of the novel. I find myself questioning as often as agreeing, but it is the kind of article that provokes readers into extending their appreciation by the very act of dissenting. D.J. Dooley's chapter in *Moral Vision in the Canadian Novel* looks at first sight as though it might be nonliterary in approach.

But moral questions are so traditionally central to the novel form, and Dooley is so concerned to associate Atwood's novel with works by the masters of English twentieth-century satirical fiction (Aldous Huxley and Evelyn Waugh), that his discussion never strays far from Atwood's artistry. An emphasis on moral perspectives might be expected to become sober or even pompous in its approach; in fact, Dooley — more perhaps than any other commentator on *The Edible Woman* — insists on the comic "packaging" of Atwood's serious concerns. This is one of the most sustained and satisfying treatments, within its own limits, of a novel which, by and large, critics have not served particularly well.

These critical interpretations, then, demonstrate the richness of Atwood's text by showing how different emphases can illuminate different aspects of the book. Some are undoubtedly more legitimate than others, but an intellectually vigorous reading should be able to incorporate insights from a wide variety of approaches and so derive the utmost benefit from Atwood's impressively complex art.

Reading of the Text

SOME INTRODUCTORY FACTS

In the introduction to *The Edible Woman* that she wrote for the Virago reprint (collected for Canadian readers in *Second Words*), Margaret Atwood points out that the novel was written "in the spring and summer of 1965, on empty examination booklets filched from the University of British Columbia" (*Second Words* 369). She had spent the academic year 1964–65 teaching English and composition at that university, and the examination books in question are now preserved in the Atwood collection of the Thomas Fisher Rare Book Library at the University of Toronto. She also notes that the idea for the culminating scene that provides the book with its title occurred "a year earlier" when she was gazing "at a confectioner's display window full of marzipan pigs," an experience that proved stimulating because, as she remarks, she had "been speculating for some time about symbolic cannibalism" (369). This would presumably have been in Toronto, since we know that between 1963 and 1964 she was working for a Toronto market-research company.

During that year in Toronto, she celebrated her twenty-fourth birthday.[4] For the previous two years she had been engaged in graduate studies in English at Harvard University, and she was now getting her first extended taste of life in what is sometimes described as "the real world" by working for the firm that clearly provided some of the inspiration for Seymour Surveys. Novels are rarely autobiographical in any exact sense, but by the same token they are seldom totally independent of their writer's personal experience. It is interesting to note, then, that *The Edible Woman* is a novel about a woman who works in the area of market research, and that it includes within its boundaries a critical presentation of what Atwood has elsewhere called "the pompous, neurotic graduate student ethic" (Miner 190). We also know that, the previous year, she had met James Polk, whom she would marry in 1967. It would be improper, to say the least, to posit any connection between the Marian/Peter relationship and Atwood's own personal life — Marian and Peter are imaginative creations with their own characters and emotional tangles — but the twenty-four-year-old Atwood would naturally have been considering at least the possibility of marriage in the not-too-distant future. It is hardly surprising, then, that to marry or not to marry should be a major question at this time; indeed, Atwood once admitted that this novel "expresses her own early fear of marriage" (Miner 189–90).

According to Atwood's own account, the original version of the novel was completed late in 1965 and submitted to "a publisher who'd displayed some interest in my previous book" (*Second Words* 370). (This is clearly Jack McClelland of McClelland and Stewart.) No definite decision was made for eighteen months, at which time Atwood made inquiries and discovered that the typescript had been mislaid. This would be in the summer of 1967, by which time Atwood was a very different person from the little-known writer who had submitted the text. In 1966, her first major book of poems, *The Circle Game*, had appeared, and by the following summer it had won the Governor General's Award for poetry. Atwood, within the small world of Canadian writing, was now a celebrity. As she tells the story, McClelland agreed to publish the novel, without having read it, "out of sheer embarrassment" (370).

During the following year, the academic year 1967–68, Atwood was teaching literature at Sir George Williams University (now a part of Concordia University) in Montreal. At this time, the more experienced writer decided to make a systematic revision of the text. (It is interesting to note that the Atwood papers in Toronto contain a file of suggestions about revision by Clark Blaise, a fellow teacher at the university, at that time unknown but later to become an important Canadian writer himself.) The main changes consisted in the substitution of a completely rewritten opening, the introduction of what is now chapter 23, and some considerable changes in the last two chapters. Elsewhere, changes were generally stylistic, and resulted in a sharpening of the wit and a tighter control over the effect of individual scenes. Names (of characters and places) were altered, and some details were brought up to date. At the end of chapter 29, for instance, the "familiar bridge with subway cars moving on it" (265) is a revised wording since, when she originally wrote the book some two years earlier, the east-west line of the Toronto subway system was not yet in operation, and there were no subway cars on the Bloor-Danforth bridge. These circumstances, incidentally, explain one social-historical anomaly in the text. Certain details of updating firmly set the novel in the late 1960s (the book appears to follow the 1968–69 calendar, though it also fits that of 1963–64), but, for those who remember the 1960s, the emotional "feel" of the book reflects the earlier years when Atwood was writing the first version. There is, for example, no hint of the radicalism and unrest that marked the later years of the decade.

The Edible Woman eventually appeared, more than four years after Atwood had begun to write it in British Columbia, in the late summer of 1969. It had the distinction of being published in Canada, Great Britain, and the United States, the respective publishers being McClelland and Stewart in Toronto, André Deutsch in London, and Little, Brown in Boston. The novel's popularity is sufficiently indicated by the fact that it has never been out of print since that time. Various paperback reprints have appeared over the years, including the McClelland and Stewart New Canadian Library edition employed here (see "Note on Editions and References" above). In New York the Popular Library produced an edition in 1976, and in 1978 Bantam-Seal issued an entirely reset version for distribution in both Canada and the United States. Both these versions contain a slightly larger number of pages. The London Virago edition (1980) reproduces the original 281-page text.

One oddity of the original editions concerns the spelling of the protagonist's surname. This appears five times in the text (on pp. 13, 20, 126, 168, and 223). On the first two appearances the name appears as MacAlpin, on the last three as McAlpin. (Confusion is increased in the New Canadian Library introduction where it becomes McAlpine!) The explanation for this inconsistency is revealed by an examination of the manuscripts and typescripts now held in the Atwood collection at Toronto. In the original manuscript, the heroine's name was either Moorhouse or Moorehouse. The alteration came late. In a typescript of the final version, the new pages read MacAlpin, but some sheets (lightly corrected) were incorporated from an earlier draft. Here the new name has been written in by Atwood, and the spelling variant McAlpin came into existence at that time. It is difficult at this stage in time to decide whether one version has better claims over the other. In the Popular Library text, someone has noticed the anomaly and "MacAlpin" has been adopted consistently. However, since "McAlpin" appears to be the slightly later choice, has a slight numerical majority, and seems to be the favoured version employed by commentators, I am using it here.

CHAPTERS 1-5: "FEELING UNSETTLED"

The first surprising feature of this book that we are likely to notice is its title: how can a woman be edible? This question is not resolved until the end of the novel, but the disconcerting implications, along with the epigraph derived from *The Joy of Cooking*, alert us to the importance of food imagery in the book and may well lead us to take note of an otherwise harmless-sounding reference to breakfast in the opening paragraph. In fact, we shall find that the characters in this novel spend a high proportion of their time at meals; breakfasts, coffee-breaks, lunches, teas, dinners, and parties follow each other at almost indecent speed.

"I know I was all right on Friday when I got up . . ." (11). The opening sentence is arresting. We do not know who is speaking, but we know from the verb tenses (present followed by past) that, at the time of speaking or writing, the narrator is no longer "all right." Atwood is employing here one of the conventional tricks of the popular novelist's trade that is recommended in every handbook of fiction writing; she plunges us *in medias res* — into the middle of the action — without identifying the speaker (initially, we do not even know whether it is a man or a woman), without explaining where or when the scene is taking place, or offering any clues about the kind of story we are to expect (will it be funny or serious? a novel of character or of action? realistic or a fantasy?).

Whenever we begin a novel, we start reading slowly and carefully because we need to get our bearings. In the opening pages of this book, we gradually register answers to the questions raiscd in the previous paragraph. We soon realize that the setting is contemporary — or, at least, contemporary with the time of writing — since we are in a world of electric toothbrushes and the conversation, with its vernacular expressions ("soggy," "drooled," "so bloody one-track" [11]) and the apparently uninhibited life-style that it reflects (". . . most men look at something besides your *teeth*, for god's sake" [11]), clearly mirrors our own world. The subsequent exchange with "the lady down below" (13) — which unostentatiously reveals the sex and surname of the narrator — further suggests that an uneasy relation between generations is involved, an awkward clash of fashions and assumptions. The "high heels expected by the office" (12) are not designed for easy negotiation of narrow and slippery stairs with loose stair-rods. The landlady is associated with causes that the two younger women consider old-fashioned and outmoded (temperance, loyalty to empire), and her insistence that ". . . the district wasn't as good as it used to be . . ." (15) apparently applies an adverse value-judgement on her lodgers. By this time, we may confidently assume that the novel is going to be concerned with some serious social issues (probably social conflicts), but if we have been reading with due attention to style and tone, we shall also have decided that it is likely to treat its subject in a humorous and perhaps even satiric manner. The "lady down below" (who is never named and is referred to by this formula throughout the book) is obviously close to caricature, while the narrator's placing description of the lodging house and the sharp quality of her comments (". . . there's something cretinous about the hair-ribbon perched up on top of [the child's] gigantic body" [13]; ". . . I could feel a private atmosphere condensing around me like a plastic bag" [14]; ". . . Ainsley's floor is covered by a treacherous muskeg of used clothes . . ." [16]) all prepare us for a display of brittle wit.

Our other initial questions are answered gradually in the course of the first few chapters. We realize that Marian (her first name is established in chapter 2) is a young woman just graduated from university and now working for a market-research company. The identification of "this city" (15) is only established through inference. The name Toronto never appears in the book, but readers who know the city will pick up specific references to the Park Plaza [Hotel] (39), and the [Royal Ontario] Museum with its "gold-mosaickeddome," "spiral staircase," and "incongruous totem-pole" (182), as well as more general references to the Toronto subway and streetcar system, the city's well-known ravines, which play an important part in the climax of the story, and, of course, in terms of social character, Toronto's curious combination of the stuffily conventional and the swingingly up-to-date. Tonally, we get accustomed to a sharply observed realism, but with hints of something approaching paranoid fantasy not far below the surface. When "the lady down below" first appears complete with gardening gloves and trowel, Marian wonders "who she'd been burying in the garden" (13); a little later, Ainsley remarks: "On still nights, . . . I can hear her burrowing through the woodwork" (16); when required to sign her Pension Plan forms, Marian feels "a kind of superstitious panic" and believes that she has put her signature "to a magic document" (21). There is much that is amusing in these early chapters, but we become increasingly aware of a disturbing, even vaguely threatening atmosphere, as if characters are living in a not-quite-hermetically-sealed, unnatural world.

This impression is strengthened by the account of Marian's job with Seymour Surveys that we encounter in the second and third chapters. The more we hear of "the canned rice pudding study" (18), "the laxative survey in Quebec" (22), "the coast-to-coast instant pudding-sauce study" (24), the more ridiculous it all seems. When Marian and "the office virgins" (22) are joined for coffee by Ainsley with her story of a woman trying to electrocute her husband by short-circuiting his toothbrush, we may begin to question the sanity of the commercial world that is being presented here. Interestingly enough, Ainsley maintains that, according to her company, ". . . the thing couldn't possibly short-circuit under normal circumstances" (23). One may be forgiven for wondering whether the common phrase "normal circumstances" means anything any more. Indeed, the word "normal" develops into a disturbing leitmotif as the book progresses, and the concept of normality — including questions about what can legitimately be described as normal and how normality can be established — emerges as an important theme within the novel. Normality comes further into question when Marian's fiancé phones up with news of a friend's marriage as if it were "a national disaster" (27). The scene, to be sure, is played out as a form of farce, but it strengthens our impression that Marian inhabits a world that seems commonplace but is revealing itself as troublingly abnormal. (Could the same be said of our own, everyday, "normal" world?)

It is worth noting at this point, since words and their meanings are in question, that Marian's job involves the proper use of words:

> I know what Seymour Surveys hired me as — I'm supposed to spend my time revising the questionnaires, turning the convoluted and overly-subtle prose of the psychologists who write them into simple questions which can be understood by the people who ask them as well as the people who answer them. A question like "In what percentile would you place the visual impact value?" is not useful. (19)

There is something ridiculous about psychologists who cannot phrase questions that can be understood, and it soon becomes clear that the abuse of language in our modern commercial society is another preoccupation of the book. When Marian agrees to assist in the Moose Beer survey, she checks the telephone recording and listens to the silly advertisement jingle with its attempted psychological manipulation by means of language ("*a deep-down manly flavour*" [26], its implications connecting with the idea of an edible man). A little later, she has to answer a complaint from a woman who found a dead housefly in her cereal sample, and she realizes that in this case she must use prose not to create but to obscure meaning: "The main thing, I knew, was to avoid calling the housefly by its actual name" (28). Language and words are going to be important in this novel — as we might expect in a book by a writer who had already made her reputation as a poet. But what Atwood has established here is that her protagonist is a highly intelligent if somewhat conventionally minded woman with a sensitivity to words. It will not be surprising if, later in the narrative, she comes to ask some awkward questions about the crazy and verbally insensitive world in which she finds herself.

It is even less surprising to find chapters 2 and 3 ending on suggestions of unease. Marian confides to an office acquaintance her qualms about the Pension Plan and gets the response: "Oh yes, it bothered me too at first . . . . You'll get over it" (24). When she leaves at the end of the day without volunteering information to the office virgins about her dinner-date, "[t]heir wistful curiosity made [her] nervous" (29). In fact, she has been invited to the home of a school and college friend, but the experience is not calculated to make her any less unsettled. The world of Clara and Joe Bates and family is presented with all the exaggerated caricature previously bestowed upon the office virgins. Indeed, this portrayal of chaotic domesticity seems to be influenced by Charles Dickens' presentation of the disorganized Jellyby family in *Bleak House*; in Dickens, Richard Carstone "saw four envelopes in the gravy at once,"[5] while in a later scene here, Marian discovers "some digestive biscuits . . . in the laundry basket" (205). Atwood paints a hilarious picture of suburban squalor, with not-yet-toilet-trained children and all the detritus of a badly run household. Marian and Ainsley negotiate "the stairs of the back porch, which were overgrown with empty bottles of all kinds, beer bottles, milk bottles, wine and scotch bottles, and baby bottles," and eventually find the again-pregnant Clara who "in her seventh month . . . looked like a boa-constrictor that has swallowed a watermelon" (31). The simile is brilliantly comic, but Marian ultimately contrasts this grotesque figure with the "fragile" Clara she had known at high school: "In that classroom full of oily potato-chip-fattened adolescents she was everyone's ideal of translucent perfume-advertisement femininity" (36). Here, as so often in this novel, the humour suddenly darkens. If the office virgins and rice-pudding studies represent the commercial world as vacuous pointlessness, the Bates family offers a daunting picture of marriage and maternity. The office virgins hope after a few years of work and travel to "get married and settle down" (22); Marian, who is only beginning to question the world as she has found it, expects to do the same. The prospect, however, is anything but appealing.

Marian and Ainsley return to their apartment, but the disturbing events of the day are not yet over. While they are enjoying a late-night drink, Ainsley suddenly announces: "I'm going to have a baby." Knowing her care in sexual matters, Marian doesn't believe this, and Ainsley clarifies the situation by saying: "I mean I'm going to get pregnant." To which Marian replies: "You mean you're going to get married?" (39). The routine is amusing — especially since Ainsley actually means that she wants a child without the inconvenience of a husband. The exchange demonstrates the basic differences in attitude between the two women. We can now appreciate why "the lady down below" has decided that Ainsley "isn't respectable" whereas Marian is (13). A spectrum of moral viewpoints is becoming manifest. At one extreme, we have the Victorian narrow rectitude of "the lady down below"; at the other, there is Ainsley with her "liberated" views derived from some dubious anthropology courses at her college. And in the middle is Marian, who "knew Ainsley was wrong" but finds it difficult to argue with someone who "sounded so rational" (43). Ainsley calls her "a prude" (42), but that is too strong a term — the genuinely prudish "lady down below" would be horrified to learn that the respectable Marian drinks as well as Ainsley and even engages (as we shall shortly learn) in premarital sex. Nonetheless, her life-style, though "liberated" by the standards of much of mid-1960s Toronto, is clearly quite conventional when compared with Ainsley's. Can it be that, having retained a social and moral conscience, she is an obsolete and endangered species?

The fifth chapter closes with Marian's one-sentence paragraph: "I got into bed, feeling unsettled" (43). We can understand why. What began as a normal working day has been gradually but relentlessly undermined. On waking, she had been feeling "more stolid than usual" (11), but a series of events have combined to challenge her assurance. For the reader, however, these opening chapters have created an intriguing complexity. Most of us will recognize aspects of our own world in this narrative, but it is viewed from an unusual angle. We are amused at the comic effects and, if we have been reading carefully, are impressed by the crisp cogency of Atwood's style. Here is a novelist, we feel, in full control of her material. At the same time, there are hints of possible awkward challenges to assumptions that have been accepted as having a solid basis. Eager to read on, we are nonetheless somewhat apprehensive that our conventional attitudes may be jolted; we too find ourselves "feeling unsettled."

CHAPTERS 6–12: "ON AN EMOTIONAL BRINK"

At the opening of chapter 6, Marian leaves her narrow world of apartment, office, and friends' home to undertake her assignment in the preliminary Moose Beer survey. She gets off to a bad start by encountering first a "temperance" (by which they mean teetotal) couple and then a lecherous male who attempts a sexual pass. There is nothing particularly unlikely about this, but it is worth noting that these incidents represent extreme dualities — unreasonable sensual restraint on the one hand, immoderate sexual licence on the other. We realize at this point that, with the exception of Marian herself, Atwood is dealing here — as classic comedy has always dealt — with traditional and simplified types. Most obvious in this regard are the three carefully categorized office virgins already introduced, Millie with her "girl-guide practicality," the socially conscious Lucy, and Emmy "the office hypochondriac" (22). The "lady down below" clearly fits here as the classic strait-laced landlady, and so does Clara in her role as ever-pregnant wife, and Ainsley as the (albeit idiosyncratic) radical feminist. We shall soon be meeting others — notably Leonard Slank, the compulsive seducer, and Peter, the rising lawyer with his desperately balanced images of smart man-about-town and intrepid hunter. This is what we expect in a traditional comedy of manners, and it would be foolish to criticize Atwood for lack of depth in the presentation of her characters when her perfectly justifiable concern is with a grotesque world of superficial values and responses. Marian's first two interviews fit neatly, and artfully, into this pattern.

But Marian, like the reader, is in for a shock with her final interview; Duncan (though neither protagonist nor reader learns his name until nearly halfway through the novel, and his surname remains a blank) eludes all categories. An emaciated, unpredictable graduate student in English, who is apparently twenty-six though he looks only fifteen (49), he is described as "a starved buddha burning incense to itself" (51) — a paradox indeed, since the Buddha advocated the renunciation of selfish desire. On the other hand, he was famous for seeing through the duplicities of this world, and Duncan on a comic level performs a similar function. He proceeds, while ostensibly responding with fascination to the Moose Beer jingle, to subject it to the devastating critique which it so obviously deserves. Marian asks for his response to "Deep-down manly flavour": " 'Sweat,' he said, considering. 'Canvas gym shoes. Underground locker-rooms and jock-straps' " (52). More pointedly, another part of the commercial patter, "Healthy hearty taste," reminds him of "cannibal stories" (53), and so revives our half-forgotten questions about "the edible woman." To add to all this, however, he proves unreliable and even duplicitous himself. After first claiming to qualify for the survey as a "seven to ten bottles per week" man (49), he suddenly announces, "I never drink the stuff" (54), though this is almost immediately negated when his roommates return from shopping and offer him a beer (55). For Marian, the whole interview becomes disorienting. As soon as she sees him, she realizes that the questionnaires she was carrying "had suddenly become unrelated to anything at all, and at the same time obscurely threatening"; she even feels "a slight sensation of alarm" when she steps over the threshold (49). There is a distinct sense of unreality about the whole scene, a hint of fairy tale with Duncan as ambiguous dwarf and the strangely furnished apartment as a kind of enchanted, possibly sinister castle. Duncan's impact is bizarre but unforgettable. We never meet the temperance couple or the lecher again, but we know that Duncan will reappear.

In the next chapter, the tone shifts violently yet again. Marian sets off for her boyfriend's apartment, which turns out, on the fairy-tale level, to be another (even more sinister) magic domain, the one completed suite in an as-yet-unfinished building that forms part of a vast high-rise complex. Atwood devotes considerable attention to the description of this building, and it is tempting to explain this as part of her passion for accurate topographical detail. One soon senses, however, that she is making a profound comment on the social history of Toronto in the 1960s. It is a city caught in a vigorous but uncomfortable period of change. Side by side with the old-fashioned, solid houses of the kind in which Marian lives — engaging if decaying vestiges of what used to be called "Toronto the Good" — are beginning to appear these new representatives of a totally different kind of city. Peter (who, a generation later, would be classified as a "yuppie") is given an appropriate habitat, and it is significant that, for all her ostensibly modern ways, Marian lives in a part of Toronto that belongs to the past. It would be excessively pompous to speak in terms of symbolic space, yet, with her deft artistic instincts, Atwood carefully provides even her type-characters with appropriate settings.

Peter is described as "ordinariness raised to perfection" (61), a conventionally acceptable figure, obviously at the start of a successful career (". . . his is a small firm and he's rising in it like a balloon" [57]). When Marian arrives, he is taking a shower, and one of his type characteristics throughout the novel is that he always smells of soap. Another side of his character, however, is represented by his "collection of weapons: two rifles, a pistol, and several wicked-looking knives" (59). His recently married friend, we recall, is significantly named "Trigger."

As soon as Peter emerges, he invites Marian into the bathroom, and they engage in an absurd sex-scene in the bathtub. One gets the impression that the two are becoming real-life characters in a shoddy commercial film, that Atwood is parodying the clichés of popular art while at the same time demonstrating how, in a world of commercialized entertainment as well as commercialized everything-else, individuals are likely to act out the patterns of movie stereotypes. After the expected climax, Peter asks the inevitable question, "How was it for you?" (62), and then bites Marian's shoulder "as a signal for irresponsible gaiety." The scene ends as follows:

> I bit his shoulder in return, then, making sure the shower lever was still up, I reached out my right foot — I have agile feet — and turned on the COLD tap. (63)

One is tempted to add either the stage-direction "Curtain" or the film-direction "Cut."

This is Atwood in a farcical mood (consider the

implications of "I have agile feet"), and it depends for its effect on a delight in sheer artifice. We become aware at this point of the unabashed contrivance that is evident throughout the book. However "realistic" parts of it may be (the descriptive detail, and — within the limits of exaggerated caricature — the credibility of the characters), this is contrived art, and an appreciation of the novel presupposes our responding to the consummate artistry of Atwood's performance. Here, when she closes a scene on a theatrical climax, we begin to realize how slickly traditional the book is in its basic form and structure. *The Edible Woman*, we might say, is a book about convention and the challenge to convention that manifests itself within the complex art of living. Yet its "heroine" (the standard word seems half apt, half inappropriate) is herself the product of an artistic convention, and Atwood both exploits and makes fun of fictional conventions in the writing of the book. This is at once a witty and engaging (if disturbing) novel, and a dazzlingly precocious exercise in the art of fiction.

Marian's situation reaches the point of crisis in the eighth and ninth chapters. She has decided to take Peter to meet Leonard Slank (the college friend with a reputation for seduction), and the party is gate-crashed by Ainsley who is clearly looking Len over as a possible collaborator in her child-making. Here we have a parody version of the standard fictional device of tracing the varied fortunes of two couples (generally during the period of courtship) and comparing and contrasting their procedures. Marian feels ethically responsible for any Len/Ainsley relationship and finds the situation distasteful. This feeling is exacerbated when Peter and Len find common ground in hunting and shooting with guns and cameras. Peter hunts wild animals and Len young girls, but Marian begins to feel herself as the potential prey of both. She overhears Peter's description of shooting a rabbit:

> "I picked it up and Trigger said, 'You know how to gut them, you just slit her down the belly and give her a good hard shake and all the guts'll fall out.' So I whipped out my knife, good knife, German steel, and slit the belly and took her by the hind legs and gave her one hell of a crack, like a whip you see, and the next thing you know there was blood and guts all over the place." (69)

Len "bared his teeth"; Peter considered it "funny." Marian now indulges in one of her recurring fantasies in which she visualizes the scene but "couldn't see the rabbit" (69) — for the obvious reason that she recognizes herself as the victim (notice the feminine pronouns in Peter's speech). Here the supposedly "feminist" aspect of the book is most pronounced, yet Atwood has typically complicated the issue. If Peter is playing up his role as macho hunter in an expression of solidarity with Len the womanizer, we know that Ainsley is assuming an innocent-little-girl role for an anything but innocent purpose, since Len, in this case, appears doomed to become her victim.

In terms of fictional conventions, the scene develops at this point from a comedy of manners into a sequence allied to Gothic terror. The words "horror," "panic," and "menace" occur (70–71), and when they all leave the bar at closing time and agree to adjourn to Len's apartment, Marian, in a sentence that gains added emphasis by closing the eighth chapter, "let go of Peter's arm and began to run" (71). The following chapter begins with an eerie effect as she lopes along the dark streets pursued by Peter in his car and Len on foot in what becomes a surreal and macabre love-chase. "All at once it was no longer a game. The blunt tank-shape [of Peter's car] was threatening" (73). Hunting imagery gives way to that of a military operation; this is the war between the sexes. The effect is only momentary, and the pursuit soon collapses into a parody of a Hollywood police-chase, but it leaves a memorable impression. While Marian's behaviour appears irrational, Peter's action is recognized even by Marian herself as "the logical thing to do" (73). When she is eventually caught, Peter's voice seems "normal" again, and Len wonders if she is "the hysterical type" (74). We begin to suspect, however, that the apparently firm boundaries that claim to separate the normal from the irrational are beginning to blur. Can it be that Marian, in words she has applied earlier to Duncan, is "tottering on an emotional brink" (53)?

In Len's apartment another "irrational" scene occurs, though this time at an almost farcical level. Bored by the talk of cameras and lenses, Marian succumbs to an irresistible urge to hide in "the dark cool space between the bed and the wall" (75). She gets stuck, has to be rescued, and emerges "furred and tufted with dust" (78), looking ridiculous. I say "*almost* farcical" because within this bizarre incident Marian has come to an important decision. In going under the bed, she sees herself as "underground" (76), "below ground" (78), and in this situation she begins to see her way more clearly: "I was evading reality. Now, this very moment, I would have to face it. I would have to decide what I wanted to do" (77). And, a little later: "I had broken out; from what, or into what, I didn't know" (78). This is a more serious, more mature Marian than we have met before; for the first time she is beginning to view her life independently, without assuming that the ways of her society are necessarily "normal" and right.

For the second time that night, Marian runs away — into what promises to be a violent thunderstorm. Here inner and outer weather are threatening to correspond in the sanctioned way of romantic convention. Peter catches up with her in the car and offers her a lift home, which she is realistic enough to accept. The complexities of the situation become evident when he complains of her behaviour: "Ainsley behaved herself properly, why couldn't you? The trouble with *you* is . . . you're just rejecting your femininity" (80). By this time Marian realizes that all she is rejecting is his and society's male-influenced idea of femininity. Again she sees him as the archetypal hunter, looking at her "as though he was taking aim" and stepping "murderously" on the accelerator (81). In his anger he skids onto private property and leaves two deep gouges on the owners' lawn. This, too, he considers "funny" (81), and Marian begins to question the moral values of this supposed lawyer.

The scene is clearly moving to a climax and, as always in *The Edible Woman*, this climax is both conventional and unexpected. As they wait outside her apartment "in the centre of the storm" (82), Peter suddenly proposes. In realistic terms, this is unlikely, given Marian's embarrassing behaviour throughout the evening, but Peter is, as we might say, on the rebound from Trigger's defection into marriage, and romantic conventions virtually demand a passionate avowal within this scene of tempest. The storm obeys its cue. As soon as he suggests marriage, a "tremendous electric blue flash, very near, illuminated the inside of the car" (83). Such atmospheric contrivances are standard devices, but it is difficult to escape the conclusion that Atwood is alluding here to the well-known scene in Charlotte Brontë's *Jane Eyre* in which Rochester proposes. (In that novel the proposal scene takes place under a chestnut tree "in peace," but as soon as Jane accepts him the tree "writhed and groaned" and a storm breaks. Next day, it is reported that the tree "had been struck by lightning in the night, and half of it split away."[6] The marriage, of course, is — at least initially — doomed.) Once again, Atwood is interweaving — intertextually, as they say nowadays — the conventions of society and the conventions of art in a way that challenges both.

Chapter 10, set in Marian and Ainsley's apartment the following morning, is straightforward and need not detain us long. One detail, however, that seems innocent enough at first reading, takes on considerable importance later. Marian goes to the refrigerator and finds herself wondering "whether [she] could face an egg" (83). This is the first hint of her subsequent inability to eat, and it comes, significantly enough, as soon as she has accepted Peter's proposal of marriage. In addition, Ainsley's strategy with regard to Len is here made clear, and this relationship is contrasted with Marian and Peter's when the latter arrives to initiate their life as an engaged couple. More significant is the juxtaposition of this conventional scene between the two lovers, which ends on Marian's expression of a sanctioned deference ("I'd rather leave the big decisions up to you" [90]), with her visit to the laundromat and her second meeting with Duncan. Here again Atwood skillfully changes fictive gears. If we read this chapter with too heavy an emphasis on realism and credibility, the coincidence of meeting Duncan again is troubling. But Duncan exists as the opposite to all that Peter represents. He is not a "realistic" figure, and Atwood never tries to make us believe in him in realistic terms. He is, in fact, as close to a supernatural character as one can imagine without entering into the alien mode of the ghost story. We first met him in the mildly surreal setting of the graduate students' apartment; here we find him in an equivocal no-man's-land. A laundromat is, after all, a locus for the homeless and the transient, a place for those who lack family and roots. Atwood presents Duncan and Marian staring at "three glass windows, like portholes or aquaria" (94). If, under Len's bed, Marian was "underground," she is now in a strange dimension under the sea.

And here, without warning, Duncan embarks on a speech that introduces a central image of physical and psychological entrapment:

> "Once I went to the zoo and there was a cage with a frenzied armadillo in it going around in

> figure-eights, just around and around in the same path . . . . They say all caged animals get that way when they're caged, it's a form of psychosis, and even if you set the animals free after they go like that they'll just run around in the same pattern." (95)

The image recurs twice a little later (98–99, 108); it is powerful because it sums up Marian's own dilemma. After feeling trapped the previous day, she determined to "break out," but, as soon as Peter proposed, she not only returned to the cage by accepting him but reverted to the traditional pattern of wifely behaviour ("I'd rather leave the big decisions up to you"). Duncan's function in the novel gradually emerges as the voice of Marian's instincts and intelligence, as a kind of spirit-guide from a ghostly underworld who can dispense a paradoxical wisdom. He presents his own situation in relation to Trevor and Fish, the two graduate students with whom he shares the apartment — "They think I'm mad. . . . I think they're mad" (99) — a situation that Marian is being led to recognize as her own — even as *la condition humaine*. And once again he raises the issue of cannibalism, though this time (a further indication that Atwood's attitude cannot be contained within a feminist aesthetic) the cannibal is female rather than male: "Florence Nightingale was a cannibal, you know" (100). But Atwood does not leave the scene on this semi-Gothic note. Once Marian and Duncan have completed their laundry, they leave to go their separate ways, but the conventional movie-style imperatives take over. Such scenes *must* end with physical contact, so ". . . we dropped our laundry bags to the sidewalk and took a step forward. I found myself kissing him, or being kissed by him, I still don't know which" (100). In terms of fictional convention, this is comic parody; in terms of Marian's life it is complicating and disturbing — "the plot thickens," to quote the conventional cliché.

The next chapter opens with a one-line paragraph: "So here I am" (101). The verb-tense has changed significantly from past to present (this is the only chapter in the book in the present tense). Sherrill Grace complains, unconvincingly, that this chapter, "though intriguing, is less successful both formally and thematically. It disrupts the temporal consistency of the narrative and confuses the irony of the story" (*Violent Duality* 90). Both disruption and confusion are, of course, deliberate. It constitutes, in fact, the most movingly immediate scene in a novel that is, in the main, comically detached. Marian is now forced to analyse her actions and feelings. The outcome sounds significant: ". . . now I've gone over it all in my mind I see that my actions were really more sensible than I thought at the time. It was my subconscious getting ahead of my conscious self, and the subconscious has its own logic" (101). This appears promising, but the immediate result is (for the thoughtful reader) a surprise — Marian's conclusion that the acceptance of Peter was "a very good step to take" (101–02). She seems to be reverting to her conventional assumptions, accepting the sanctioned pattern "to marry someone eventually and have children, everyone does" (102). She decides, indeed, to have either two or four, since "three is a bad number" (102) — interesting insofar as Clara Bates has announced her intention to stop at three (34). Life, Marian asserts, "isn't run by principles but by adjustments" (102). At the same time, she has to admit that she "still can't quite fit in the man at the laundromat." She persuades herself that "... there's little chance of my ever running into him again ...," but we as readers know better. Part One comes to an end with her realization that she has "a lot to do" (103). We suspect, however, that the "adjustments" she needs to make will be both radical and painful.

CHAPTERS 13–20: "OUT OF CONTROL"

The first two words of Part Two, which begins at chapter 13, are "Marian was ... " (107). We notice immediately that, while the tense has reverted back from present to past, the narration has turned from first to third person. The effect on the reader is somewhat disorienting, all the more so since to switch narrative modes in this way is a violently unconventional procedure in a novel that has so far been conspicuously sensitive to the dictates of convention. It is important, however, that we realize precisely what is implied by this effect. Atwood has not switched from Marian's viewpoint to that of a detached narrator; rather, Marian has resolved to view her own actions from an external perspective. As Jayne Patterson has observed, ". . . the split voice . . . allows her to objectify her experience, to stand back from herself as it were, and it is through this distancing process that she is able to emancipate herself from her initial role as victim" (151). The point is made within this narrative section itself: "She had caught herself lately watching herself with an abstracted curiosity, to see what she would do" (173).

The thirteenth chapter itself returns us to the brittle comedy-of-manners world and is set for the most part in the slightly batty environment of Seymour Surveys. The turmoil of the office, we notice with interest, recalls Duncan's image of the frenzied armadillo to Marian's mind. She later announces her engagement to the office virgins over lunch in a fairly predictable scene, though a further hint of the future crisis is made manifest when she notes with surprise that she isn't hungry. The most notable event occurs when she learns about "the Underwear Man," who poses over the telephone as a Seymour Surveyor and asks increasingly intimate questions of the female respondents. Mrs. Bogue charitably observes that ". . . he's probably some nice ordinary man, perfectly harmless . . ." (116), while Lucy categorizes him as "one of those sex-fiends" (117). Marian not only finds herself making a strange reply to Lucy — "Maybe it all proves that some sex-fiends are very nice normal people" (117) — but later finds herself speculating whether the Underwear Man and Peter may not be one and the same: "Perhaps this was what lay hidden under the surface, under the other surfaces, that secret identity which in spite of her many guesses and attempts and half-successes she was aware she had still not uncovered . . ." (118). The fact that she can entertain this possibility about her fiancé shows how, deep down, she is not fully convinced that acceptance of his proposal was "a very good step to take."

Later in the day, Marian discovers that Ainsley has planned Len's seduction for that night and chosen Marian's bedroom as the suitable locale. She agrees to spend the evening at a late movie where she encounters Duncan yet again. His eccentric behaviour (unseen in the dark theatre, whispering "pumpkin seeds" into Marian's ear so that she thinks she is hallucinating) persuades her that she is "finally going mad . . . like everybody else" (126). The following day, he rings her up with the bizarre request that she bring him some laundry to satisfy his obsession with ironing. She immediately agrees, even though it means that she must postpone a dinner with Peter. It is as if she is being drawn, mysteriously, into Duncan's orbit. In another fantasy, at the hospital where she has been visiting Clara (who has now given birth), she meets a masked, antiseptic, vaguely familiar doctor who appears to be a projected image of Peter. Her office workers consider her someone who "never lets herself get out of control" (108), but neither Marian nor the reader is so sure.

The ironing scene at Duncan's is another episode of eerie but possibly meaningful unreality. At first he shocks her with another of his duplicities. After offering a complicated story about a broken mirror (in which Marian cannot see herself), he adds: "I suppose you believed all that .... That's the trouble with people, they always believe me" (140). It is as if, like Francis Bacon's Pilate in a famous essay, he jestingly asks, "What is truth?" and does not stay for an answer.[7] A little later Duncan announces (but can he be believed?): ". . . I come from the underground . . . " (141). Later still, he offers an enigmatic observation that brings together, as we later realize, two of the major thematic concerns in the book: "Production-consumption. You begin to wonder whether it isn't just a question of making one kind of garbage into another kind. The human mind was the last thing to be commercialized but they're doing a good job of it now . . ." (143). The preoccupation with eating (consumption) that has already been established is here linked with the idea of commercialism, itself prominent in Marian's market-research work and her fascination with advertisements. As the novel proceeds, we become aware, thanks to Duncan's hint, that the book is calling into question many of the basic assumptions of our consumer society.

Some critics, notably Ildikó de Papp Carrington in " 'I'm Stuck,' " have emphasized the fact that Marian puts on Duncan's dressing-gown while he irons her blouse and that he then remarks: ". . . you look sort of like me in that" (144). This is commonly linked with theories of the double or *Doppelgänger*, and Carrington even more specifically argues for an intertextual allusion to Joseph Conrad's novella "The Secret Sharer." Such connections are possible, but, in my view, they can be exaggerated and argued too solemnly. More to the point is the fact that, by this manipulation of plot, Marian is visually linked to Duncan rather than to Peter. This leads conveniently to the scene in the next chapter where Marian is having her postponed dinner with her fiancé. It begins with Ainsley's description of Peter as "nicely packaged" (146), and this idea will soon be brought within the imagistic magnetic field of the consumer society. Seymour Surveys is preoccupied, like most commercial enterprises, with problems of packaging, and the application of the phrase to Peter is both complicating and disturbing. This in turn leads up to the climax of the scene. The engaged couple are both eating filet mignon when Marian, watching Peter "operating on the steak" (notice the verb and its image-connection with the doctor in the hospital), suddenly realizes that the meat was "[p]art of a real cow that once moved and ate and was killed" (151). The process is disguised when, in supermarkets, ". . . they had it all pre-packaged in cellophane . . ." (151). She can eat no more, and she gets the definite intuition that this reaction will continue; she ends the chapter by fearing that she may starve to death.

Several weeks pass before the opening of the eighteenth chapter, and during this time the reaction has not only continued but spread. "The day after the filet, she had been unable to eat a pork chop . . ." (152), and the list of forbidden foods (what distinguishes "the non-devourable from the devourable" [153]) increases. But (and here the imagery begins to cohere) the only alternative to animal foods seems to be "the cellowrapped and plasticoated and cardboard-cartoned surrogates" (155). Ironically, as T.D. MacLulich was the first to point out, Marian's challenging of what is "normal" leads her to an extreme in artificiality. Marian, MacLulich writes, "is using the products of the consumer society to sustain a rebellion which is ostensibly directed against that very society" (122). At the office Christmas party she chooses a jelly sandwich and is disturbed by conversation among the office virgins about a woman who "just stopped *washing*" (165). As so often before, she begins to feel "dangerously close to some edge" (171) and immediately encounters Duncan again in the death-like environment of a snow-covered city park. She nuzzles against him in an effort to get warm; once again, he provides a need (human but not, as yet, sexual) that she cannot find in Peter.

At the opening of the next chapter, "Marian was walking slowly down the aisle, keeping pace with the gentle music that swelled and rippled around her" (172). But it isn't a wedding march, and she isn't in church. The aisle belongs to that modern secular social-centre, the supermarket, and Marian is choosing food (mainly vegetarian) for a dinner to which Clara and Joe Bates as well as Peter have been invited. She is mesmerized by the way the goods are presented, "deceptively-priced or subliminally-packaged" (172), some vegetables "in bags or rubber-banded bunches," tomatoes "prepackaged in cardboard and cellophane boxes of four" (173). Her problem is to devise a dinner where her now narrowly restricted eating habits would not be too conspicuous, and she settles on a casserole, with plans to conceal uneaten meatballs under unfinished salad. But, as we might have expected, she is in for a shock: "She became aware of the carrot" (178). Atwood has skillfully manipulated our responses here. There are comic aspects to the development; at the same time, we know — better, indeed, than Atwood and her readers did in the mid-1960s — that anorexia is a serious illness, and we are naturally drawn in sympathy to Marian's plight. In literary terms, we are faced with an intricate effect where the standard categorizations ("comic" or "serious"; "sympathetic" or "detached") are no longer useful.

The dinner is not a success, but at this point Atwood juxtaposes Marian's crisis with Ainsley's. The latter's sexual strategy with Len has been successful, and some weeks earlier she had been pronounced pregnant. She had not been present at Marian's dinner because she was attending a Pre-Natal Clinic, from which she returns "on the verge of tears." She has just heard a lecture from a psychologist on the importance of "a strong Father Image in the home": ". . . it makes them *normal*, especially if they're boys" (181). Ainsley is convinced (without evidence) that her child will be a boy and is now terrified that he will grow up a homosexual. Atwood's structural plotting now becomes clear. Whereas Marian began as a "respectable" young woman contrasting with Ainsley as independent rebel, Marian is now moving towards the officially abnormal while Ainsley is drawn back to the conventional. This again is one of the standard patterns of classic comedy. A famous instance is Jane Austen's *Pride and Prejudice*, in which (I am, of course, simplifying a more intricate situation) Mr. Darcy must temper his pride and Elizabeth Bennet conquer her prejudice before they can be united at the end of the book. The pattern is essentially artificial, but this should not deter us. The experienced reader will appreciate the artistry of the novelist while at the same time responding to the satire on commercialism and consumerism and the human dilemma facing Marian as protagonist. A talented novelist should be able to sustain many notes at the same time. At this stage in *The Edible Woman* Atwood has proven herself as comedian, satirist, social commentator, skilled practitioner in the art of fiction, and, above all, as a versatile entertainer with a capacity to broaden our understanding.

CHAPTERS 21–25: "DO YOU THINK I'M NORMAL?"

"They were holding hands as they went up the wide stone stairway . . ." (182). These are the opening words of chapter 21, but "they" refers not, as we might naturally expect, to Marian and Peter but to Marian and Duncan. The "wide stone stairway" belongs to the Royal Ontario Museum, a favourite Atwood locale. One of her most memorable poems, "A Night in the Royal Ontario Museum," appeared in *The Animals in That Country* less than a year before the publication of *The Edible Woman* (though it was almost certainly written after the novel), and a number of the scenes in a later novel, *Life before Man*, take place within its walls, since two of the three main characters are museum workers; more recently, Atwood contributed an article, "The Royal Ontario Museum," to a coffee-table book entitled *Ontario* (1983). The speaker in the poem imagines herself locked overnight in the museum; it is described as a ". . . crazed man-made / stone brain" (20), where she wanders endlessly among the artefacts, one of which is

> . . . a skeleton child, preserved
> in the desert air, curled
> beside a clay pot and a few beads (21)

— an image duplicated in the novel. The conception of the poem recalls Marian's fantasy of being "trapped past closing time" in the supermarket (175), but the emphasis is not so much on a Gothic-terror image of entrapment as on the way in which we are all trapped in a time-slot and surrounded by scattered objects representing past ages. In *Life before Man*, Atwood concentrates on the prehistoric section relating to dinosaurs, the obvious reference being to a whole era of life-forms discarded and superseded by the pitiless powers of evolution. In the article, where both Egyptian mummies and dinosaurs are singled out as the favourite galleries of her childhood, the museum is seen more positively as an imaginative world of wonders, "the quintessential time capsule" (11).

Although Marian and Duncan climb *up* the spiral staircase to reach the Ancient Egyptian section, in the topsy-turvy world of *The Edible Woman* the journey clearly represents a symbolic visit to the underworld, a descent to the world of the dead. Atwood has remarked in an interview that the scene in the sixth book of Virgil's *Aeneid*, in which Aeneas goes down to the underworld to learn secrets from the dead, has been important to her (Sandler 16). Within the novel, we feel that Marian has found in Duncan an ideal guide to this nether world. It is, as always with Duncan, a world of equivocation. On the way, he shows little interest in her marriage, though he remarks that ". . . it sounded evil to him . . ." before directing the conversation back to "the complex and ever-fascinating subject of himself" (184). At first this sounds appallingly egoistic; on further reflection, however, we may come to suspect that Duncan, as guide, is indirectly teaching Marian an all-important lesson in self-responsibility: that she must ultimately think for herself and make decisions for herself.

Duncan first shows her his "favourite mummy-case" (186), a brightly coloured but indeterminate figure that Marian assumes is female but, according to Duncan, is "supposed to be a man" (187). In the world of death, gender seems unimportant. Duncan moves on to another case, opened so that the mummified body is visible inside. This provides Duncan with material for two "lessons." His first comment, "[v]ery well preserved," reminds us that mummification is the art of packaging raised to the highest level of perfection. Duncan underlines this point by making a brief but emphatic comparison with contemporary funeral practices: "They could never do a job like that now, though a lot of those *commercial* body-snatchers pretend they can" (187; my italics). At the same time, he offers some gnomic comments about life and death. After observing that he sometimes wants to live forever, he refers immediately to "Mutabilitie" (the paradoxical state of perpetual change), and in answer to Marian's complaints about his morbidity remarks: "What's wrong with death? . . . There's nothing morbid about it; we all do it, you know, it's perfectly natural" (187). Since what is "natural" and "normal" is a concern at the heart of the book, this is an observation worth pondering.

Marian's quick retort that it is not natural to like death causes Duncan to repeat a sentiment he has expressed before. " 'Don't take me seriously,' he said. 'I've warned you about that' " (187). This is a signal that, once again, Atwood is about to switch gears from the serious to the comic, though by this time it should be clear that in Atwood, as in most comic artists of importance, the comic and the serious are ultimately inextricable. Claiming that he wants to show her his womb-symbol, he takes her to the same exhibit that was described in the poem, a stunted, crouched figure, resembling the body of a child. There is no question here of gender identification — the narrator refers only to "it" — and in this case birth (Duncan's womb-symbol) and death (a skeleton) have disturbingly coalesced. Like the wise men in T.S. Eliot's poem "Journey of the Magi," Marian (and, doubtless, the reader) thought that birth and death were different; here the distinction seems to have evaporated. (As Duncan has remarked in the laundromat scene, words "are beginning to lose their meanings" [96].) Duncan now clinches his enigmatic point by introducing physical love into the debate. With the curious comment, "Don't worry. . . . I'm not going to return from the tomb," he bends to kiss her, only to be interrupted by the forces of respectable Toronto in the shape of a uniformed guard who announces that ". . . kissing in the Mummy Room is not permitted" (188). The whole scene dissolves into farce (literally, since interrupted dalliance is one of the conventional staples of farce), but Marian returns from the underworld with some problematic but intriguing clues to the challenges of living in the present.

A brief scene in the Museum Coffee Shop conveniently furthers the plot, since they meet Trevor and Fish there, and Marian is duly invited back to the graduate students' apartment for one of Trevor's gourmet dinners. Earlier in the chapter Marian has suspected that Duncan's companions thought that she was "trying to gobble [him] up" (185). Clearly, the image of eating and food is coming to the forefront again, and when Marian confesses her eating problems, Duncan throws out another tantalizing hint: ". . . you're probably representative of modern youth, rebelling against the system; though it isn't considered orthodox to begin with the digestive system" (192). The idea of an orthodox rebellion contains some built-in ironies; here, as before, Duncan is offering a not-too-serious suggestion that is worth considering but should not be accepted as gospel. Its relation to any interpretation of the novel and its meaning is of interest, however, because early in the next chapter, which takes place in the students' apartment, we are confronted, as a kind of pre-prandial intellectual cocktail, with Fish's bizarre account of his theories about *Alice's Adventures in Wonderland*, which is also Atwood's hilarious parody of the excesses of contemporary literary criticism.

This passage is a piece of consummate comedy in itself, but it also has numerous and complex ramifications. Several commentators have made the point, even in the titles of their articles, that Atwood is not averse to inserting allusions in her work as a whole, and especially in *The Edible Woman*, to the intricate and profound "nonsense" writings of Lewis Carroll. Robert Lecker entitles his study of her first three novels "Janus through the Looking Glass," John Lauber's article on *The Edible Woman* is called "Alice in Consumer-Land," while the chapter in Barbara Hill Rigney's book that discusses this novel is called "Alice and the Animals." This is but one indication that critics tend to see the mention of Lewis Carroll's comic but disturbing masterpiece as an important clue to the interpretation of the book.[8] And there is obviously much to be said for this view. Certainly the present chapter leads into a scene with unmistakable connections to the Mad Hatter's tea-party, and the commentators are right to point out how eating and drinking are also significant motifs in *Alice's Adventures in Wonderland*, and how the juxtaposition of the real world of Victorian England with the strange underworld that exists down the rabbit-hole has profound equivalences in *The Edible Woman* (consider the numerous references to rabbits in this book, from Peter's hunting story onwards). In addition, both books share a remarkable blending of the comic and the horrific. Moreover, further connections can be (and have been) made. Fish calls *Alice* "a sexual-identity-crisis book" (193), and this too is a categorization that can be applied to

Atwood's novel. Again, Fish argues against the view that "by the end of the book [Alice] has reached anything that can be definitely called maturity" (194). This has led a number of commentators to deliver the same judgement on Marian, though I suspect that Duncan might have some complicating remark to make about the meaning and relevance of "maturity."

At the same time, to place too much importance on references that appear in what is unequivocally a deconstructing parody is a somewhat dangerous procedure. It is worth remembering that, like all the characters in the novel except Marian and Duncan, Fish is a two-dimensional comic type. This means that he represents in exaggerated form a particular viewpoint that, because it is isolated, and offered as *the* approach instead of one possible approach, becomes excessive and therefore ridiculous. It is also a warning — one which, I am bound to repeat, too many critics have ignored — that any literary commentary that takes itself too seriously and neglects the comic element within the whole critical proccss is doomed to absurdity. This passage *is*, I would argue, a clue to reading the book, but (like Duncan's pronouncements) it is an enigmatic clue, one that suggests what should be avoided rather than what should be followed. (I also feel bound to make an observation here about Atwood's own literary criticism: how, after producing this passage, she could go on to write *Survival*, her influential but critically dubious "thematic guide to Canadian literature" [to quote its subtitle], with all its — one assumes — unintentionally comic victim positions and its narrow categorizations, is beyond my power to explain.)

The dinner that follows works up to an artificial climax faithful to the traditions of farcical comedy. Comment is hardly necessary on the sequence of events that leads up to the collapse of the dinner table and to Marian's being caught by Trevor in the act of throwing to Duncan a chunk of unwanted meat that ends up on a pile of term-papers. The scene does, however, provide an opportunity to make a comment on Atwood's structural expertise. This is the first time that we have seen Duncan for any length of time within his own milieu and as part of the graduate-student trio. The threesome may cause us to remember the three office virgins at Seymour Surveys. With Fish as an obsessed specialist in womb-symbols, Trevor a gourmet-cook homosexual, and Duncan a sexually ambiguous child-man, they constitute a suitable equivalent of male grotesques. A critic insensitive to the implications of the literary-critical parody already discussed might be tempted to launch out at this point into a learned discourse on the significance of trinitarian structures. That would, of course, be absurd, but it is in keeping with the terms of Atwood's text to remember that the novel itself has a three-part structure, and that Clara and Joe have three children, though we should also remember that, as I have already noted, Marian (in defiance of Pythagoras) considers three "a bad number" (102). Why this numerological concern? Real life does not conform to such mathematical precision. I suggest that the prime reason for Atwood's triple emphasis is that she wants us to recognize artifice as artifice, since one of the pleasures that we derive from reading fiction is an appreciation of the means that have made the novel possible. *The Edible Woman* may ultimately have something to say that is applicable to "real life," but it is not in itself real life; Atwood is insistent that we think clearly (as Marian needs to think clearly) and that we learn to recognize the novel for what it is.

Artifice is equally conspicuous in the next chapter. Marian now realizes that she must "face up" to her eating problem, and her main worry is highly significant: ". . . what was essentially bothering her was the thought that she might not be normal" (203). She therefore resolves to approach the three people she knows best — Ainsley, Clara, and Peter — and to ask them: "do you think I'm normal?" (204, 206, 207). The answers, as we might expect, vary according to the character of the speaker, which means that they are of little use to Marian. Ainsley, obviously drawing on her recollections of college psychology, asserts that "[n]obody is normal" (204); Clara calls her "abnormally normal" (206); Peter pats her on the rump (that revealing male-chauvinist gesture) and leers that he finds her "marvellously normal," though ". . . she didn't mean it that way." There is a sense in which, so far as the ideas that generate the novel are concerned, this is a central chapter, since it identifies the concept of normality as a central concern of the book. Interestingly enough, examination of the manuscript and subsequent drafts reveals that this chapter was added at a very late stage of composition. It is a sequence more important for the central themes of the novel than for its plot. It presents a psychological rather than a situational climax. The next step in Marian's development will be to question the assumptions about "normality" that are accepted unthinkingly by the society in which she lives. (A concern for what is normal, incidentally, runs throughout Atwood's work; both word and concept are especially prominent in the later novel *Bodily Harm*.)

The next two chapters focus on the preparations for Peter's engagement party. Here Marian is being "packaged" out of all recognition, and the scene in the hairdresser's shows Atwood at her most sharply satiric. This scene also brings together much of the telling imagery that she has already employed. When all the technology is in place, Marian's head resembles "a mutant hedgehog with a covering of rounded hairy appendages instead of spikes" (209); we are reminded perhaps of Duncan's image of the frenzied armadillo. More often, however, the imagery is drawn from the clinical, industrialized, "air-conditioned-nightmare" side of modern city life. The hairdresser becomes a "doctor," Marian is required to lean against what she sees as an "operating-table," and she begins to think it would be a good idea to "give anaesthetics to the patients" (209). Later, she is returned to "the doctor's chair to have the stitches taken out," the whole process is seen in terms of an assembly line, and the hair-dryer looks like an "electric mushroom." Moreover, after a nurse has "pronounced her dry," Marian is taken back along "the gently-fryingline of those who were not yet done" (210), so the recurrent cooking image is also included. The descriptions are unquestionably humorous, but under the humour we detect a bitter attack on the absurdities of contemporary fashion.

The rest of the chapter is taken up with a confrontation between Ainsley and Len, since Ainsley (growing more conventional as Marian becomes more questioning) is now pressuring Len into marrying her. She is deservedly unsuccessful, and the chapter ends with "the lady down below" receiving a blasting harangue from the departing Len (Atwood's version of Shaw's "not bloody likely" in *Pygmalion*) which, if we are at all familiar with the traditions of farcical comedy, we should have known would occur at some point. In the next chapter, the essentially artificial finishing touches are put on Marian by Ainsley, and in order to strengthen herself for the ordeal of the party, Marian impulsively invites some guests of her own — the office virgins, Clara and Joe, and even the graduate-student trio. Atwood is here contriving the traditional "big scene" in which all the characters in the book will be incongruously mixed, a sure fire recipe for situational disaster and a comic climax. Events are clearly working up to crisis-point. Predictably, the landlady appears to give the lodgers notice, but the chapter ends on the logical culmination to Marian's problem that most readers, in my experience, seem to miss. As she takes one of her vitamin pills, she suddenly begins to look more closely and sees them as "hard-cased brown seeds": "I wonder what they grind up to put into these things, she thought as she swallowed" (224–25). The implication is surely clear: now even vitamin pills, the lowest common denominator of food, will be "forbidden."

CHAPTERS 26–29: "GETTING AS FAR AS DUNCAN," OR "TONIGHT'S THE NIGHT"

As in the previous scenes, we are aware at this point not only that the plot is working up to a resolution of some kind but also that the ideas and imagery dominating the book are beginning to converge. Marian arrives early at Peter's apartment so that she can help him in any last-minute preparations. But the place is "meticulously neat as always" (228) and Peter "seemed to have everything well under control" (230). The contrast with Marian, whose apartment is now cluttered with unwashed dishes and who is clearly losing control of her psychological stability and her bodily responses, is obvious. When Peter is himself ready, all the imagery of war and hunting rushes back into his vocabulary: ". . . it's almost zero-hour, but before they come I'd like to get a couple of shots of you alone . . . . Could you just stand over there by the guns . . . ?" (231–32). It is an unpromising beginning to the party, since the references concentrate all Marian's doubts about Peter's character.

I have already noted that Atwood is here contriving a scene in which all the main characters in the book will come together with uncomfortable but doubtless comic results. If we have been reading carefully, however, we will have noticed that, with the obvious exception of "the lady down below," Leonard Slank is the only prominent character who has not been invited to the party. Needless to say, he arrives with Clara and Joe, and it takes little literary perception to forecast that he will be conspicuous in the ensuing climax. But it is Duncan who makes the first significant gesture. Arriving with Trevor and

Fish, he eyes Marian in her artificial finery and sees the party with clear-eyed objectivity: " 'You didn't tell me it was a masquerade,' he said at last. 'Who the hell are you supposed to be?' " (239). Independent as always, he refuses to enter, and announces his intention of returning to his appropriate habitat, the aquaria-like laundromat. At the crucial moment in the book when she presumably needs him most, Marian is deprived of her guide.[9]

Ainsley creates the first incident by rowing with Len, smashing her glass, and, in the embarrassed silence, asserting: "Len and I have a marvellous announcement to make . . . . We're going to have a baby" (240). This is both conventional and a defiance of convention. Formal announcements are standard at parties — it is entirely possible that some official recognition of Marian and Peter's engagement was going to be made on this occasion — but an announcement of having a baby without a socially approved marriage-ceremony deliberately flouts conventional practice. But more (worse?) is to come. Len goes one better, announces a pre-birth christening and (again reproducing the sanctioned routines of slapstick comedy) anoints Ainsley by emptying his beer stein over her head. At this point the pace gets fast and furious, and Fish — against all the rules of probability, but Atwood has now abandoned herself to pure artifice — comes into his own. Deserting symbolic wombs for an actual pregnancy, he performs a Sir Walter Raleigh act of traditional "courtesy" by removing his sweater, drying her off, and patting her belly while speaking in a voice "heavy with symbolic meaning" (241). By this time, any convention is acceptable, and we have little difficulty in recognizing a latter-day rendition of love at first sight. (Linda Hutcheon has noted perceptively ["From Poetic" 18] that Fish's action casts Ainsley in the incongruous role of Venus rising from the sea that he has earlier invoked at the graduate students' dinner.)

But a comic scene in Atwood, as we have seen on several occasions, is always liable to turn into something horrendous and threatening. After a fantasy sequence in which Marian desperately tries to envisage a "normal," non-violent Peter, she is suddenly confronted with him once again as the camera-shooting hunter. In an at least partly self-induced Gothic climax, she screams hysterically and realizes that she "had to get out before it was too late . . . . It all depended on getting as far as Duncan: he would know what to do" (244). The manner of escape may be humorous — her garish and uncharacteristic scarlet dress ironically becomes protective camouflage in a society where garishness is the norm — but the seriousness of her flight is not in question. Once again (another trio in this novel of trios) she realizes instinctively that she must run for her life.

When she finds Duncan at the laundromat, he

greets her as "the Scarlet Woman herself" (247), and the comment is more than a mere visual analogy. Whereas Marian has run to him for guidance and protection, as soon as they meet the roles are reversed, and she begins to look suspiciously like a seducer who has tracked down her prey. The pattern of production and consumption, consumer and consumed, is continually working both ways. Duncan now accepts the inevitable: "tonight's the night" (247). The scene in which they go out in search of "some sort of hotel" (248) — Marian's euphemism — is a brilliant composite of mixed genres inviting mixed reactions, at once a parody of the "daring" low-life movie, a frightening sequence illustrating modern alienation, a study in the grotesque (Duncan and Marian constitute the most oddly matched couple imaginable), and even a scene of moving human pathos slightly off-key. Atwood has achieved such superb control over the effects to be obtained through her art that she can not only ring instant changes from the comic to the serious, from the realistic to the grotesque, but also create scenes that contain balancing elements of both. By the time they find a room, of course, she is moving towards a richly comic effect.

The stage is now set for the obligatory sex-scene that is traditionally expected at this stage in such a book; but the heroine seems to be getting into bed with the wrong person, and the issue is (to say the least) in doubt. The presumably escalating climax is punctured by a classic instance of Atwoodian incongruity. "Well, what do we do now?" asks Duncan. "You must know" (251). Unforecastable to the last, he is apparently more interested in a vulgarly commercial ashtray (a "Made In Japan" souvenir of Burk's Falls) and in Marian's girdle (an object he has only seen "in the ads" [252]) than he is in Marian herself. But the mood changes yet again. "She walked doggedly towards the bed, gritting her teeth" (253) is a sentence which can be read as black comedy, bleak horror, or desperately human irony, according to the mood and capacity of the reader. Ideally, perhaps, it can be read as all three simultaneously. At first, it seems as if the scene is doomed to anti-climax — after half an hour Duncan comments: "It's no use. I must be incorruptible" (253) — but then comes a particularly surprising moment in this novel of surprises. Suddenly, Duncan takes control, and acts with assurance and even confidence. Although the suggestion that he strokes her "as though he was ironing her" has absurdly comic associations, we realize that Duncan has something to teach Marian even here. As he approaches her like an animal, "curious, and only slightly friendly" (254), the protean quality of the scene becomes clear. The act of sex can be comic, sublime, threatening, ridiculous, unpredictable. Marian enters a world where hunter and hunted, victor and victim, are no longer adequate words. What begins as a half-comic, half-sordid encounter in a shabby, commercially rented room becomes a complicated and complicating experience.

Atwood's capacity to follow, and yet to parody, convention is nowhere more clearly indicated than in the tantalizing hiatus between the end of chapter 28 and the beginning of chapter 29. The effect is blatantly imitative of the old-style movie with its fade-out just before the sex-scene begins and its picking up of the strands on the following morning: "They were sitting in a grimy coffee-shop around the corner from the hotel" (255). Atwood is reminding us, by reverting to what might seem for the unthinking avant-garde to be a hoary and hypocritical convention, that the perfunctory bump-and-grind with its Brobdingnagian enlargements of human bodies now standard in the commercial sex-film is itself a convention. (This is perhaps alluded to by Duncan when he complains: "There's just altogether too much flesh around here. It's suffocating" [253].) But she is also suggesting that even the old and apparently superseded conventions can be revived successfully to make a witty and profound point. Atwood is presupposing an intelligent and sophisticated readership at this stage in the action, one that can respond to a joke about media conventions all the more appreciatively because it realizes that it has been led — by standard "packaging" — to expect something else.

The scene in the hotel was decidedly ambiguous. In traditional comedy, love is supposed to resolve all problems, but the mechanical and laborious sexual act implied here seems closer to a demonic parody of love. This becomes clear when Marian now discovers that her intimation about the vitamin tablets at the end of the twenty-fifth chapter is indeed fulfilled. She can eat nothing for breakfast: "It had finally happened at last then. Her body had cut itself off" (257). At the same time, one suspects that, as so often when she meets Duncan, an indirect lesson has been learned, and this is borne out by his decision to take her for a walk. Once again he becomes purposeful and authoritative: "He seemed to know where he was going .... He was leading her. He was in control" (259). His destination proves to be one of the Toronto ravines, which provides an ideal realistic-and-symbolic setting for Marian's final and decisive lesson from her mentor.

It is worthwhile digressing at this point to discuss the significance of Atwood's use of the ravine as a peculiarly apt setting here. During the 1960s, when exciting developments were taking place in Canadian literature (with Atwood in the vanguard), Torontonians were beginning to become aware of the literary and symbolic possibilities of the natural physical features of their city. A year after the publication of *The Edible Woman*, the novelist and short-story writer Hugh Hood published an article in the Toronto *Globe and Mail* entitled "The Ravines and Bridges of Hugh Hood's Toronto." (This was later revised and retitled to become the name-essay in his 1973 essay-collection *The Governor's Bridge Is Closed.*) In it, as in his later novel *Reservoir Ravine* (1979) among others, he draws upon his childhood memories of the city. Throughout his life he has thought of "the bridges and ravines [as] the most important imaginative properties on the Toronto scene," and he adds: "I still feel the same way."[10] The ravines have earned a dubious reputation in Toronto life. After Hood published the original newspaper article, he reports in *The Governor's Bridge Is Closed*, he received a number of similar responses from women readers: "When I was small my mother used to tell me, 'Don't go and play in the ravines, darling; there are bad men down there.' But I always went anyway" (8–9). Atwood was well aware of this reputation. Duncan remarks: "The old drunks come down here and sleep under the bridges and the kids play here too" (261). Moreover, readers of *Lady Oracle* (1976) will remember Joan Foster's adventures with the bullying Brownies in one of the ravines and her ambiguous encounter with "the daffodil man." A comparable ravine scene appears in *Cat's Eye* (1988). For Hood, however, the ravines have a more classically symbolic role: "I still think that Toronto is a city where sooner or later you find yourself going down into a dark place in the ground" (9).

This is the sense in which Atwood employs the ravine here. On the one hand it is an accurate presentation of a well-known part of Toronto which, thanks to the readily identifiable "familiar bridge with subway cars moving on it" (265), the Bloor-Danforth bridge across the Don Valley, is an easily recognizable location in the real world. But the scene is equally open to interpretation as another version of the "journey to the underworld" motif that we have met before. Atwood conjures up an eerie sense of a mysterious subterranean city with awesome features. Duncan points out a sombre-looking building as the brickworks (Hood describes his almost fatal, real but also symbolic near-fall over a cliff close to the brickworks in the essay from which I have just quoted) and even speaks of "a prison down here somewhere, too" (262). It is a wintry landscape with unmistakable suggestions of a country of the dead, the kind of setting that Duncan seems to find congenial. As always, the advice he gives is indirect and enigmatic. When, however, Marian suggests that she should perhaps consult a psychiatrist, he is unambiguously against it: "Oh no, don't do that. They'd only want to adjust you." To which she replies, significantly: "But I want to be adjusted . . ." (263). Adjustment is only desirable, we realize, if the social world involved is itself normal. But this is precisely the assumption that the novel is challenging, and if "society" is recognized as profoundly abnormal, then psychiatric adjustment is both superfluous and pointless.

Duncan's next response is much more characteristic. Marian finds herself asking the standard question that Peter had asked her after their session in the bathtub: "How was it for you last night?" (263). His reply — "fine; just as good as usual" (264) — throws into doubt all her previous assumptions, and challenges the reader as well as Marian to reconsider the whole scene in the hotel bedroom. When, one wonders, is Duncan telling the truth, and when is he being maddeningly duplicitous? As the narrator remarks, reproducing Marian's thoughts: "There was the possibility also that this revelation was just as fraudulent as so much else had been" (264). Duncan's point seems to be, however, that life is always deceptive and equivocal, that he is offering valuable practice in interpreting and surviving in a duplicitous world. When Marian observes that she must now decide what she is going to do, his reply is honest and trustworthy in its refusal to offer advice that cannot properly be given: "Don't ask me, that's your problem. . . . [Y]ou'll have to think of your own way out" (264). Marian asks him to return and talk to Peter, but he refuses; all he can do is to show her the way back to the upper world. At the end of the chapter, Marian sees him appropriately as "a dark shape against the snow, crouched on the edge and gazing into the empty pit" (265).

Although Duncan appears once more in the closing pages of the novel, his crucial function within the book is effectively over at this point, and it is fitting that we pause here to consider his character and significance in the fiction as a whole. Critics have tended to respond to him with suspicion or distaste. Alan Dawe calls him "unappetizing" (second page of unpaginated introduction) — which at least exploits the dominant imagery of the book; to Sherrill Grace he is "self-indulgent, . . . sloppy, ineffectual, childish" (*Violent Duality* 92–93); Ildikó de Papp Carrington finds him not only "procrastinating" and "effeminate" (" 'I'm Stuck' " 84) but even "mentally sterile" (72)! These evaluations seem to me not only inaccurate and unhelpful but, at least in the last quoted instance, totally misguided. Others are more helpful. Jerome H. Rosenberg considers him "slovenly" but is prepared to grant that he is "possibly [Marian's] salvation" (97). In my view, however, the most accurate assessment yet provided in print is D.J. Dooley's:

> This man is anything but ordinary . . . . His response to the world of commerce . . . is gamesmanship . . . . The difference between him and most other people is that he is quite aware that he is playing a role, whereas they

> are falling into roles without knowing it. Just as he is capable of looking at his own situation objectively, he is capable of analyzing his society. He prefers a literal wasteland to the wasteland of the modern commercial world . . . . In other words, his response to being as it is defined in the modern mercantile world — fitting into the cycle of production and consumption, making one kind of garbage into another — is to come as close as possible to not-being. (142)

Duncan may be an irritatingly paradoxical character, but he is advocating the paradoxes of duplicity as a possible way of coping with the world. Earlier in this section, I described him as a "mentor," a word derived from a character in Homer's *Iliad* and *Odyssey* famous for his role as faithful adviser. "Faithful" may not be the right word for Duncan, and his advice may be indirect, but in a frighteningly threatening world he performs an equivalent function. He is the most intellectually probing of all the characters in the novel and the only character besides Marian herself who is more than a comic type. While he is hardly attractive, and can be infuriating, he seems to me a splendidly complex creation, one of the most original creations in Canadian fiction. Perhaps the heart of his paradox can best be hinted at by paradoxically applying to him a remark used of one of the world's most profound but also enigmatic mentors: "He saved others; himself he cannot save" (Matt. 27.42).

CHAPTERS 30–31: "ONLY A CAKE," OR "BACK TO SO-CALLED REALITY"

The first thing we notice in the thirtieth chapter is that, when Marian returns to the upper world, the roles hitherto played by herself and Peter have been reversed. As soon as he phones, we are told that it is Peter who had "lost control" (265), a nice instance of the way in which a repeated word has the capacity, when used in a new context, to make a significant point about the action as a whole. Similarly, when Marian makes her second visit to the supermarket, she goes in a very different frame of mind and displays a very different pattern of behaviour. Jayne Patterson has established the point in an elaborate and exhaustive stylistic analysis, but it is sufficient here to note that Atwood achieves the effect consummately with the deft use of a single adverb: "In the supermarket she went *methodically* up and down the aisles . . ." (267; my italics). We realize at once that this is a new Marian.

The narrator tells us that Marian has decided on a

mode of action to deal with the problem of Peter, "[s]ome way she could know what was real: a test, simple and direct as litmus-paper" (267). We take note of a necessary decisiveness here, though Duncan should now have persuaded her that "real" is as slippery as any other word with which to try to categorize the manifold aspects of the modern world, and that, whatever happens, it is unlikely to be "simple and direct." In fact, Duncan has been consistently instructing her in the ways of indirection, and Marian's test turns out to be appropriately equivocal. It soon becomes clear that she has decided to bake a cake, a curiously traditional action but one in keeping with her continual desire to act as a normal woman. But this conventional act soon reveals itself as anything but normal. Our first clue to the new development comes unobtrusively in an odd use of a pronoun. When the baking is almost complete, Marian asks herself: "What am I going to put her on?" (268). The cake (note "her") has acquired a gender. When Marian proceeds to mould "her" into the image of a woman, we register the fact that this normal domestic object is turning into a bizarre self-image and that the dominant images in the novel are coming together in a grand culmination. As Linda Hutcheon has pointed out, the woman-cake represents a "reconciliation of the hunger and love polarity" ("From Poetic" 20). Moreover, in giving the image a dress of bright pink made from icing that incorporates red food-colouring, Marian is transferring the artificial trappings that transformed her in the party-scene from herself to the cake. In addition, when she starts to mould the cake, Atwood uses the phrase ". . . she began to operate" (269), returning once more to the doctor-hospital imagery we have already noted, but with a significant difference since, if baking is the conventional female action, operating is a traditional male preserve. Above all, the moulding of the cake into the form of a woman is a supreme instance of "packaging"; the commercial image is being used here (a tactic Duncan has been advocating all the time) to throw out a challenge to the mercantile consumer-society world that Peter represents.

How seriously are we to take this image of an edible woman? The question itself may be loaded since, in the hands of a skillful creative artist, comedy itself can be the medium for serious (but never solemn) commentary on life and manners. At all events, Marian herself, despite the purposeful confidence of her action, becomes uncertain at this point. She has "a swift vision of her own monumental silliness, of how infantile and undignified she would seem in the eyes of any rational observer" (270). But is Peter, who is cast unknowingly as the judge in this eccentric test-case, a rational observer? When he arrives, she seems prepared to accept him in this role:

> Now that she had seen him again, the actual Peter, solid as ever, the fears of the evening before had dwindled to foolish hysteria and the flight to Duncan had become a stupidity, an evasion; she could hardly remember what he looked like. Peter was not the enemy after all, he was just a normal human being like most other people. She wanted to touch his neck, tell him that he shouldn't get upset, that everything was going to be all right. It was Duncan that was the mutation. (271)

Nonetheless, the next sentence begins: "But . . . ." Marian is coming to realize that she is split between two world-views, between the conscious and the subconscious worlds represented by Peter and Duncan respectively. (The protean, intangible, "non-realistic" quality of Duncan becomes clearer as soon as we regard him as a representative of the mysterious, impalpable, "underground" subconscious world.) The split is also one between the rational and the irrational, the logical and the illogical — though, as we have already noted as early as the twelfth chapter, Marian had sensed that ". . . the subconscious has its own logic" (101). It is also a split between the daylight world of ordinary life and the baffling night-world of dream and nightmare. Atwood has always been interested in dichotomies — her first book of poems, *Double Persephone*, is named after the character in Greek mythology who has to split her time between this world and the underworld, between light and darkness. It is interesting that the poet-turned-novelist makes use of similar imaginative structures in her fiction.

Atwood does not give us a direct account of the actual confrontation between Marian and Peter. After she offers him the cake there is a section-space, the next paragraph beginning: "When he had gone. . . ." All we know is that he hasn't eaten the cake and that their relationship has terminated. At first sight, the hiatus seems a mistake, an evasion, but on further reflection it becomes clear that the details of their conversation are less important than the significance and implications of the whole sequence. "As a symbol," Marian tells herself, the cake "had definitely failed" (271) — but one wonders. Indirectly, the gesture appears to have succeeded. Now Marian sees Peter clearly for what he is — not a potential husband but a two-dimensional advertisement-cliché: "She could see him in her mind, posed jauntily in the foreground of an elegant salon with chandeliers and draperies, impeccably dressed, a glass of scotch in one hand; his foot was on the head of a stuffed lion and he had an eyepatch over one eye" (272). Atwood is alluding to contemporary glossy advertisements for whisky and men's shirts, standard during the 1960s in such magazines as the *New Yorker*. Moreover, Marian realizes immediately that the spell of anorexia has been broken. "Suddenly she was hungry. Extremely hungry" (271). As soon as she has broken off her engagement with Peter, her body reverts to normal responses. In addition, as soon as this happens, the cake ceases to be regarded as a symbol, failed or otherwise, and becomes "only a cake" (273). It is no longer an edible woman but an edible cake; Marian does the normal thing, since she is hungry, and begins to eat.

Because it takes on particular importance as providing the title for the novel, the woman-cake has stimulated a high percentage of the critical commentary so far expended on this book. This is understandable enough. If the "meaning" of the novel is to be found anywhere, it will surely be located in an explanation of the title-image. Atwood herself, characteristically, is most interested in the technical effect of the image within the fiction. In the interview with Graeme Gibson she describes Marian's action in moulding the woman-cake as "preposterous," but adds, "as all pieces of symbolism in a realistic context are" (25). The commentators, in general, have been more ponderous. With the exception of the novelist Jane Rule, who dismisses the idea of the cake as a profound symbol — "Fortunately, it is a resolving trick more than anything else" (44) — critics have taken the image very seriously indeed, and have read into it a variety of intellectual and psychological interpretations. While I would not be quite as dismissive as Rule, I sympathize with her reluctance to attach a great deal of interpretative baggage to a work that is, after all, a comedy. Rule, however, goes too far to the other extreme, arguing that the novel is "*farce* rather than satire," that it is "not meant as a vehicle for too much serious criticism of consumer society" (44), and eventually summing it up as "the puff pastry it claims to be — a treat of wit and invention" (45). Is it possible, I wonder, to have one's cake and eat it? Is the book, indeed, a series of witty variations on that proverbial theme?

That the book *is* a comedy, Rule's "treat of wit and invention," can hardly be in doubt. That it is also a passionately committed exposé of the world of packaging and consuming (processes that expand from merchandise to include human beings as well) seems, *pace* Rule, equally certain. As to the existence of any profound meaning, the issue is less clear. Where most commentators on the cake-symbol go wrong, I believe, is to assume that it must have one meaning only, and also to assume that a novel's meaning will be the same kind of meaning as that of a philosophical treatise or a political tract. It is essential to note how the cake has decidedly different meanings for all the characters who come into contact with it. For Marian it begins, as we have seen, as "a test" and ends as "only a cake." For Peter, we may reasonably infer, it is a symbol of her madness — or, at least, of her unsuitability as the wife of a rising young lawyer. (In the early manuscript version, indeed, this is made quite explicit.) To the now conventional Ainsley, who enters with Fish not long after Peter's departure, it is an indication that Marian is "rejecting [her] femininity" (272). That Ainsley should here signal her newfound conventionality by repeating a charge previously made by, of all people, Peter (80) is a typical Atwoodian subtlety. Finally (though I am jumping here to the end of the final chapter), Duncan sees the cake for what it really is, an edible object, and in the last word of the novel he pronounces it "delicious." If there is anything that can legitimately be described as "the" meaning of the woman-cake, it is the combination of all these individual meanings which presents an appropriate emblem of the multiplicity of human reaction. (But even that sounds too solemn!)

Perhaps more important than the cake's meaning is its effectiveness. When Marian first offers it to Peter, her speech is offered as follows:

> "You've been trying to destroy me, haven't you," she said. "You've been trying to assimilate me. But I've made you a substitute, something you'll like much better. This is what you really wanted all along, isn't it? I'll get you a fork," she added somewhat prosaically. (271)

Peter is only a two-dimensional character, but we can surely absolve him from wanting to destroy her in any literal sense of the word (though Marian still believes this to be the case in the final chapter [277]). Whether he wants to do so subconsciously is a question for which there can be no satisfactory answer; whether he wants to absorb or devour her in some metaphorical way is an intriguing possibility, but equally uncertain. The prosaic anti-climax about getting the fork is Atwood's way of avoiding the danger of excessive solemnity, but we register the fact that it is also an appropriate implement on a non-symbolic level. This becomes clear in the closing sentence of the chapter, after Peter has left and Marian has regained her appetite: "She plunged her fork into the carcass, neatly severing the body from the head" (273). Comic, I suppose, but decidedly black comedy. One notes a Peter-like image of hunting ("the carcass"), and even if it's "only a cake," a suggestion of cannibalism, albeit self-cannibalism, still lingers. The cake acts as a kind of magnet attracting all the images, associations, and interpretations that come within its field. Whatever else it may suggest, the title-image performs an important function within the structure of the comedy by providing a central imagistic focus that can effect an artificial resolution.

The brief third part contains only one chapter and constitutes only five pages. The opening sentence reads, "I was cleaning up the apartment" (277), and Atwood is similarly cleaning up the accumulated clutter that has gathered around Marian's story. Most obvious, of course, is the return to the first person, another indication that Marian has regained, with variations, some of the equilibrium she enjoyed, according to her own testimony, at the beginning of the book. As she remarks, ". . . I was thinking of myself in the first person singular again . . ." (278). Most of the chapter is taken up by a final encounter with Duncan, of which more presently, but in the course of the chapter a few other details are also cleared up. Ainsley completes her transformation from feminist radical to traditional bride by departing with Fish (they have been officially married at comically high speed) for that most conventional of rituals for a North American bride, a honeymoon at Niagara Falls. (Oscar Wilde is reputed to have described Niagara as "the American bride's *first* disappointment"!) Leonard is reduced to childhood regression and is last heard of playing with the Bates children and getting into fights over toys (279–80). Marian herself, now that the engagement is cancelled, is "looking for another job" (277).

When Duncan phones, although only two days have passed since their macabre night together, Marian discovers that she has "more or less forgotten about him" (277). The implication is clear enough: Duncan has performed his function within Marian's story (one is tempted to describe him, in Robertson Davies' term, as "fifth business," but *The Edible Woman* appeared a year before Davies' celebrated novel made the phrase accessible). Their final encounter will be on very different terms. It begins with a comic reversal. Duncan rings up to find out what happened, but when Marian tells of the break-up between herself and Peter, he replies that he was really thinking about Fish. To Duncan, Fish has abandoned his responsibilities, meaning himself: "What am I going to do?" (278). There is a beautiful irony here. Marian asked Duncan the same question in the ravine only to get the reply: "Don't ask me, that's your problem" (264). It is a good reply, and Marian's answer to him is similar: " 'I haven't the faintest idea,' I said. I was irritated with him for not wanting to discuss what I was going to do myself" (278). Marian has now learned, in practice if not in theory, the art of justified selfishness. Peter's inadequacy lay, in large part, in his neglect of her legitimate interests. The tables (as so often in traditional comedy) are now turned. As Duncan puts it: "Onc of us has to be the sympathetic listener and the other one gets to be tortured and confused. You were tortured and confused last time" (278). The essential artifice of comedy is brilliantly exemplified here.

When Duncan finally arrives for tea, he is at his most enigmatic and allusive. On hearing the details of Fish's marriage and departure, he comments: "...

mankind cannot bear too much unreality" (279), a typical English-graduate-student reworking of a line from T.S. Eliot that appears in *Murder in the Cathedral* and is repeated in "Burnt Norton," the first of his *Four Quartets*: "Human kind cannot bear very much reality."[11] Both statements, one feels, are valid. But, now that Marian has taken a vital step and resolved her immediate problem, Duncan has a final surprise in store. He dismisses Marian's idea that Peter was trying to destroy her as "ridiculous": "That's just something you made up. Actually you were trying to destroy him" (280). Not content with that, Duncan goes on to assert all the possible permutations: "I was trying to destroy you. . . . Maybe Peter was trying to destroy me, or maybe I was trying to destroy him, or we were both trying to destroy each other . . ." (287). Ultimately it doesn't matter, perhaps because all are, from limited perspectives, true — and in consequence all are also false.

Clear-sighted as ever, at least when others are concerned, Duncan pronounces the final verdict: ". . . you're back to so-called reality, you're a consumer" (281). This should not be read as a glib, detachable "moral," but it points towards a reasonably obvious fact that is difficult for many people to accept — that life, like politics, is the art of the possible, and that, if one is to live in a society at all, compromises are inevitable. However accurate it may be, it is ultimately insufficient to describe contemporary society — Toronto in the 1960s or wherever and whenever readers are reading this sentence — as "a consumer society." Life itself is a consumer/consumed process; we may not live to eat, but we must certainly eat to live. The Marian who considered herself "all right" in the opening sentence of the book was not in fact "all right" because she was unaware of the realities (which can also be described as the unrealities) of her own society, and so unconscious of the fact that she was drifting into an unthinking relationship that could never ultimately satisfy her. Not only does the subconscious have its own logic, but the body has its own dramatic means of asserting its interests. (In Shakespeare's tragedy *Coriolanus*, Menenius Agrippa recounts to the rebellious Roman citizens a fable about the body and its mutinous members that rebel against the belly. The belly argues that the rest of the body depends upon the nourishment which the belly receives. The application is, of course, political — a "conservative" argument about the organic nature of society. Atwood is in a sense updating this fable in psychological terms; when the body, here the digestive system, rebels against what Marian is putting into it, it is serving notice that the demands of the inner woman must be considered.) In Duncan's most traditionally gnomic statement he instructs her, "Search your soul . . ." (280); he already knows that she has learned to search her body. He may not be able to solve his own problems ("himself he cannot save"), but he has now fulfilled his function in helping Marian in her own psychic quest. He can now enjoy his (physical) reward as the edible woman becomes a harmless item in a polite tea-party.

INTERPRETING *THE EDIBLE WOMAN*: SOME CONCLUDING THOUGHTS

Now that we have come to the last page of *The Edible Woman*, how can we sum up our reactions? What kind of a book is it? I have insisted throughout this reading that it is a comedy — and, moreover, a comedy that provides an updated but still recognizable version of the traditional form of the comic novel. This seems to me acceptable, but Atwood herself, possibly taking a leaf out of Duncan's enigmatic book, has turned this interpretation upside-down by suggesting that the novel might be considered as an "anti-comedy" (Gibson 20). In her interview with Linda Sandler in 1977 she elaborated as follows: "In traditional comedy, boy meets girl, there are complications, the complications are resolved and the couple is united. In my book the couple is not united and the wrong couple [i.e., Ainsley and Fish] gets married. The complications are resolved, but not in a way that reaffirms the social order" (13). In the earlier interview she had added a further subtlety to this basic position by observing that Peter, for all his standard physical prowess and attractiveness, is the opposite of the traditional hero: ". . . the person who embodies the restrictive forces of society is in fact the person Marian gets engaged to. In a standard comedy, he would be the defiant hero [i.e., he would defy society to gain the heroine]" (Gibson 21).

In fact, Atwood's classification is not as far removed from mine as it might seem at first sight. You cannot have an anti-comedy without a preceding, established norm of comedy against which it can be recognized and judged. Moreover, one of the traditional functions of comedy is to undermine through parody the pretensions of the serious (as the low-life Falstaff-and-Prince-Hal scenes in Shakespeare's *Henry IV* plays comment indirectly and comically on the actions of King Henry and his court). In comparable fashion, Atwood in a curiously inverted sort of way is using comic means to subvert traditional comic patterns. The result, I would argue, can be seen as both comedy and anti-comedy at the same time.

Atwood has, however, made other comments on the book and its interpretation that need to be approached more sceptically. Once, for example, when asked about the feminist aspect of the novel, she replied: "I don't consider it feminism; I just consider it social realism, and that's what things were like"

(Kaminski 8). Her reluctance to have a feminist label stuck on her novel is understandable enough; in Ainsley we have a parody of extreme feminism, and the issues that Marian faces, though presented by a female novelist through a woman's eyes, and so naturally highlighting the aspects of modern living most easily interpreted within a feminist context, affect men as well as women. Thus, even Peter can be seen as a victim of "the system" as well as Marian; his response when his friends disappear into matrimony, amusingly absurd as it is, may be seen as a comparable fear of being consumed — by women. Besides, feminists are hard pressed to explain why, if the novel is indeed "feminist," Marian feels the need of a masculine guide (however ambiguously masculine Duncan may be). Atwood's comment is best interpreted as a desperate attempt, under interview conditions, to play down a feminist over-emphasis. The remark was doubtless made on the spur of the moment, which may explain the dubious claim to "social realism." While *The Edible Woman* certainly contains elements of social realism, as I have indicated in my section-by-section commentary, the comic exaggerations are so blatant, and Atwood's flaunting of her powers of artifice so acute, that this label, on its own, is quite inadequate.

Similarly, she has offered a frequently quoted comment about the novel's ending: "The tone of *The Edible Woman* is lighthearted, but in the end it's more pessimistic than *Surfacing*" (Sandler 13–14). This attitude has (rightly, I think) surprised most critics, and it is worthwhile pausing over the comment here, since it establishes a useful point of comparison with Atwood's second novel, which appeared in 1972. Although certain thematic links can be established between the two books — both protagonists, for example, experience a radical alienation from their society — *Surfacing* is a far bleaker novel than its predecessor. Indeed, the two books provide a striking illustration of the dangers of limiting any literary inquiry to the area of subject matter. Summaries of their themes and basic structural patterns might make these novels sound reasonably similar; a response sensitive to tone and style, however, reveals them as startlingly different.

To return to Atwood's controversial comment, the tone of *Surfacing* is certainly anything but "lighthearted." The unnamed protagonist has in the course of the book been facing up to the psychological after-effects of an abortion, but by the close is poised for a return to the city in a mood that might be described as a combination of courageous determination and dour defiance. Her future, however, is decidedly uncertain. So, in a way, is Marian's, but we cannot help feeling that the experience Marian has undergone has been a maturing one, and that her compromise with a debased society is both practical and dignified. *Surfacing* is more obviously a symbolic novel and can therefore end in a more equivocal symbolic gesture. *The Edible Woman*, on the other hand, as a latter-day comedy of manners, can hardly end on anything but comic terms, however much it may diverge from an unalloyed, traditionally comic ending. In seeing this ending as "more pessimistic than *Surfacing*," Atwood seems to be re-imagining her own novel. She had been much more positive in her earlier interview with Graeme Gibson when she pointed out that, at the ending of both novels, living in harmony with the world is "seen as a possibility finally, whereas initially it is not" (27). It is a not uncommon phenomenon for novelists' attitudes to their work to change over the years, and their later judgements of earlier writings are not necessarily authoritative. D.H. Lawrence, in a famous dictum, asserted: "Never trust the artist. Trust the tale."[12] Try as I will to read this novel according to Atwood's hint, the cumulative tonal force of the book itself ultimately dictates that I end a reading of the novel on a muted, hardly optimistic, but certainly satisfying and even (in the classic sense) comic note.

What cannot be questioned, however, is the fact that in *The Edible Woman* we have a youthful, exhilarating, and intellectually challenging novel that shows one of Canada's most distinguished contemporary novelists at the height of her inventive powers.

NOTES

1 Robert Browning, "Fra Lippo Lippi," *The Norton Anthology of English Literature*, gen. ed. M.H. Abrams, 5th ed., 2 vols. (New York: Norton, 1986) 2: 1267.
2 The section devoted to "Secondary Sources" in the bibliography at the end of this book contains full details of the books, articles, and reviews discussing *The Edible Woman* that are mentioned below.
3 F.R. Leavis, *The Living Principle: "English" as a Discipline of Thought* (London: Chatto, 1975) 46.
4 In this introduction, Atwood also states that the novel "was conceived by a twenty-three-year-old, and written by a twenty-four-year-old" (369), but her arithmetic is inconsistent with the dates, which can be checked against outside sources. She was unquestionably twenty-five in the spring of 1965 when, on her own evidence, she began writing the novel; she would therefore have been twenty-four "a year earlier."
5 Charles Dickens, *Bleak House* (1853; Harmondsworth, Eng.: Penguin, 1971) 89.
6 Charlotte Brontë, *Jane Eyre* (1847; Harmondsworth, Eng.: Penguin, 1966) 280, 284, 285.
7 See the opening sentence of Francis Bacon's "Of Truth" (1625), *Norton Anthology* 1: 1673.
8 While this book was in press, Glenys Stow's article on the novel, "Nonsense as Social Commentary in *The Edible Woman*," appeared in the *Journal of Canadian Studies*. This is easily the best and most comprehensive study of the relation between *The Edible Woman* and Lewis Carroll that has yet appeared.
9 When Fish, Trevor, and Duncan appear at the door, they are accompanied by "an unfamiliar figure, probably female,

in a baggy Harris-tweed coat, sunglasses and long black stockings" (238). This mysterious creature, presumably a fellow graduate student, plays little part in the subsequent action, though we catch a glimpse of her later as she discusses death-symbols (240). Atwood has explained in the interview with Geoff Hancock (284) that this figure represents herself and was introduced as a private joke.

10 Hugh Hood, *The Governor's Bridge Is Closed* (Ottawa: Oberon, 1973) 10.

11 T.S. Eliot, *The Complete Poems and Plays, 1909–1950* (New York: Harcourt, 1952) 209, 118.

12 D.H. Lawrence, *Studies in Classic American Literature* (1923; New York: Viking, 1964) 2.

Works Cited

Atwood, Margaret. *The Animals in That Country*. Toronto: Oxford UP, 1968. Poetry.

_____. *Bluebeard's Egg*. Toronto: McClelland, 1983. Short stories.

_____. *Bodily Harm*. Toronto: McClelland, 1981. Novel.

_____. *Cat's Eye*. Toronto: McClelland, 1988. Novel.

_____. *Dancing Girls*. Toronto: McClelland, 1977. Short stories.

_____. *Double Persephone*. Toronto: Hawkshead, 1961. Poetry.

_____. *The Edible Woman*. 1969. New Canadian Library 93. Toronto: McClelland, 1973. Novel.

_____. *The Handmaid's Tale*. Toronto: McClelland, 1985. Novel.

_____. *Lady Oracle*. Toronto: McClelland, 1976. Novel.

_____. *Life before Man*. Toronto: McClelland, 1979. Novel.

_____. "The Royal Ontario Museum." *Ontario*. Toronto: Key Porter, 1983. 10–11. Article.

_____. *Second Words: Selected Critical Prose*. Toronto: McClelland, 1982.

_____. *Surfacing*. Toronto: McClelland, 1972. Novel.

_____. *Survival: A Thematic Guide to Canadian Literature*. Toronto: Anansi, 1972.

Brady, Elizabeth. "Towards a Happier History: Women and

Domination." *Domination*. Ed. Alkis Kontos. Toronto: U of Toronto P, 1975. 17–31.

Contains section on *The Edible Woman*. Nonliterary, humourless, and totally political in approach.

Bromberg, Pamela S. "The Two Faces of the Mirror in *The Edible Woman* and *Lady Oracle*." *Margaret Atwood: Vision and Forms*. Ed. Kathryn VanSpanckeren and Jan Garden Castro. Carbondale: Southern Illinois UP, 1988. 12–23.

Feminist reading emphasizing mirror imagery.

Cameron, Elspeth. "Femininity, or Parody of Autonomy: Anorexia Nervosa and *The Edible Woman*." *Journal of Canadian Studies* 20 (1985): 45–69.

Sound background on anorexia; speculative in its application to *The Edible Woman*.

Carrington, Ildikó de Papp. " 'I'm Stuck': The Secret Sharer in *The Edible Woman*." *Essays on Canadian Writing* 23 (1982): 68–87.

Argues for the influence of Joseph Conrad's "The Secret Sharer" on novel. Tends to get over-ingenious and too far away from text.

_____. "Margaret Atwood and Her Works." *Canadian Writers and Their Works*. Fiction Series. Vol. 9. Ed. Robert Lecker, Jack David, and Ellen Quigley. Toronto: ECW, 1987. 25–116.

Dogged survey of Atwood's writing, including a summary version of previous item.

Davey, Frank. *Margaret Atwood: A Feminist Poetics*. Vancouver: Talonbooks, 1984.

Both feminist and theoretical in approach. Very little discussion of *The Edible Woman*.

Davidson, Arnold E., and Cathy N. Davidson, eds. *The Art of Margaret Atwood: Essays in Criticism*. Toronto: Anansi, 1981.

Useful collection of essays on all aspects of Atwood's work; for those relevant to *The Edible Woman*, see Lecker and McLay.

Dawe, Alan. Introduction. *The Edible Woman*. By Margaret Atwood. New Canadian Library 93. Toronto: McClelland, 1973. 6 unnumbered pages.

Brief, theoretically oriented, but perceptive.

Dooley, D.J. "In Margaret Atwood's Zoology Lab." *Moral Vision in the Canadian Novel*. Toronto: Clarke, 1979. 137–47.

Thoughtful discussion of moral and ethical backgrounds to *The Edible Woman*.

Elliott, Gordon R. Rev. of *A Bird in the House*, by Margaret Laurence, and *The Edible Woman*. *West Coast Review* 5.2 (1970): 68–69.

Confused.

Gibson, Graeme. "Margaret Atwood." *Eleven Canadian Novelists*. Toronto: Anansi, 1973. 1–31.

Informative interview.

Grace, Sherrill. *Violent Duality: A Study of Margaret Atwood*. Montreal: Véhicule, 1980.

Emphasizes the binary structure in Atwood's writings; marred by errors. Contains short section on *The Edible Woman*.

_____, and Lorraine Weir, eds. *Margaret Atwood: Language, Text, and System*. Vancouver: U of British Columbia P, 1983.

Specialist articles with rigid theoretical slant (see under Hutcheon).

Greene, Gayle. "Margaret Atwood's *The Edible Woman*: Rebelling Against the System." *Margaret Atwood: Reflection and Reality*. Ed. Beatrice Mendez-Egle and James M. Haule. Edinburg, TX: Pan American U, 1987. 95–115.

Emphasizes satiric and feminist aspects.

Hancock, Geoff. Interview with Margaret Atwood. *Canadian Writers at Work: Interviews with Geoff Hancock.* Toronto: Oxford UP, 1987. 256–87.

Good interview, but only passing references to *The Edible Woman.*

Horne, Alan J. "Margaret Atwood: An Annotated Bibliography (Prose)." *The Annotated Bibliography of Canada's Major Authors.* Ed. Robert Lecker and Jack David. Vol. 1. Downsview: ECW, 1979. 13–46.

Useful, though now inevitably out of date. For later, supplementary listings, see bibliographies in Davidson, Rosenberg, and Hoy.

Hoy, Helen. "Atwood, Margaret (1939–)." *Modern English-Canadian Prose: A Guide to Information Sources.* Detroit: Gale Research, 1983. 60–75.

Useful listing.

Hutcheon, Linda. "Atwood and Laurence: Poet and Novelist." *Studies in Canadian Literature* 3.2 (1978): 255–63.

Compares *The Edible Woman* with Laurence's *The Stone Angel*, explaining differences by Atwood's experience as poet.

____. "From Poetic to Narrative Structure: The Novels of Margaret Atwood." *Margaret Atwood: Language, Text, and System.* Ed. Sherrill Grace and Lorraine Weir. Vancouver: U of British Columbia P, 1983. 17–31.

Includes difficult but thoughtful treatment of *The Edible Woman.*

Kaminski, Margaret. "Interview with Margaret Atwood." *Waves* 4.1 (1975): 8–13.

Marred by poorly prepared interviewer. Contains discussion of *The Edible Woman.*

Lauber, John. "Alice in Consumer-Land: The Self-Discovery of Marian MacAlpine [sic]." *The Canadian Novel: Here and Now.* Ed. John Moss. Toronto: NC, 1978. 19–31.

Unpolished but useful reading of the novel.

Lecker, Robert. "Janus through the Looking Glass: Atwood's First Three Novels." *The Art of Margaret Atwood: Essays in Criticism*. Ed. Arnold E. Davidson and Cathy N. Davidson. Toronto: Anansi, 1981. 177–203.

Intelligent, sensitive discussion, stressing the element of ambiguity in the early novels.

McCombs, Judith, ed. *Critical Essays on Margaret Atwood*. Boston: Hall, 1988.

Useful collection of reviews and articles, most of them previously published. Reprints articles by MacLulich and Woodcock listed below.

McLay, Catherine. "The Dark Voyage: *The Edible Woman* as Romance." *The Art of Margaret Atwood: Essays in Criticism*. Ed. Arnold E. Davidson and Cathy N. Davidson. Toronto: Anansi, 1981. 123–38.

Perceptive article, firmly setting novel within the context of Atwood's earlier work.

MacLulich, T.D. "Atwood's Adult Fairy Tale: Levi-Strauss, Bettelheim, and *The Edible Woman*." *Essays on Canadian Writing* 11 (1978): 111–29.

Oddly focused article, bringing anthropological and psychological approaches to bear, with uncertain effect. Fond of diagrams.

Marshall, Tom. Rev. of *The Edible Woman*. *Quarry* 19.3 (1970): 55–56.

Sound.

Mendez-Egle, Beatrice, and James M. Haule, eds. *Margaret Atwood: Reflection and Reality*. Edinburg, TX: Pan American U, 1987.

Collection of specialist essays (see also Greene).

Miner, Valerie. "Atwood's Metamorphosis: An Authentic Canadian Fairy Tale." *Her Own Woman: Profiles of Ten Canadian Women*. Ed. Myrna Kostash et al. Toronto:

Macmillan, 1975. 173–94.

Breezily journalistic interview-article, with some discussion of *The Edible Woman.*

Montagnes, Anne. "Two Novels That Unveil, Maybe, a Coming Phenomenon, the Species Torontonensis." Rev. of *The Lonely Ones*, by James Bacque, and *The Edible Woman. Saturday Night* Nov. 1969: 54+.

Flippant, superficial.

Moss, John. *A Reader's Guide to the Canadian Novel.* Toronto: McClelland, 1981.

Contains brief descriptive and critical account of *The Edible Woman* (1–3).

Nodelman, Perry. "Trusting the Untrustworthy." *Journal of Canadian Fiction* 21 (1977–78): 73–82.

Provocative discussion of *The Edible Woman*, raising some interesting issues without pursuing them very far.

Page, Sheila. "Supermarket Survival: A Critical Analysis of Margaret Atwood's *The Edible Woman.*" *Sphinx* (U of Regina) 1 (1974): 9–19.

The earliest article on the novel; a straightforward though somewhat simplified reading.

Patterson, Jayne. "The Taming of Externals: A Linguistic Study of Character Transformation in Margaret Atwood's *The Edible Woman.*" *Studies in Canadian Literature* 7.2 (1982): 151–67.

Lengthy stylistic analysis.

Rigney, Barbara Hill. *Margaret Atwood.* London: Macmillan Education, 1987.

Part of a "Women Writers" series and feminist in approach. Tries to link individual novels with equivalent volumes of verse.

Rosenberg, Jerome H. *Margaret Atwood.* Boston: Twayne, 1984.

Solid general introduction with brief but sound discussion of *The Edible Woman.*

Rubinstein, Roberta. "Escape Artists and Split Personalities: Margaret Atwood." *Boundaries of the Self: Gender, Culture, Fiction.* Urbana: U of Illinois P, 1987. 63–122.

Feminist-psychological study of Atwood's novels, including *The Edible Woman.* Scholarly but neglects humour.

Rule, Jane. "Life, Liberty and the Pursuit of Normalcy." *Malahat Review* 41 (1977): 42–49.

Thoughtful and solidly based discussion of *The Edible Woman*, though it underestimates social criticism.

Sandler, Linda. "Interview with Atwood." *Malahat Review* 41 (1977): 7–27.

One of the best Atwood interviews, with discussion of *The Edible Woman.*

S[kelton]., R[obin]. Rev. of *The Edible Woman. Malahat Review* 13 (1970): 108–09.

Critically uncertain.

Stow, Glenys. "Nonsense as Social Commentary in *The Edible Woman.*" *Journal of Canadian Studies* 23.3 (1988): 90–101.

Excellent discussion of the novel in relation to Lewis Carroll and nonsense literature.

Struthers, J.R. (Tim). "An Interview with Margaret Atwood." *Essays on Canadian Writing* 6 (1977): 18–27.

Good interview, but only brief discussion of *The Edible Woman.*

Texmo, Dell. "Image and Identity in Margaret Atwood's *The Edible Woman.*" *Atlantis* 2.2 (1977): 64–76.

Perceptive article, easily the best feminist reading of the novel.

VanSpanckeren, Kathryn, and Jan Garden Castro, eds. *Margaret Atwood: Vision and Forms.* Carbondale: Southern Illinois UP, 1988.

Collection of essays with feminist emphasis (see under Bromberg); also includes interview.

Woodcock, George. "Margaret Atwood: Poet as Novelist." *The World of Canadian Writing: Critiques & Recollections*. Vancouver: Douglas, 1980. 149–73.

Perceptive general discussion.

_____. "The Symbolic Cannibals." Rev. of *The Edible Woman. Canadian Literature* 42 (1969): 98–100.

Responsible, thoughtful. Incorporated into article listed above.

Updated checklists of Atwood scholarship are now published annually in the *Newsletter of the Margaret Atwood Society* (ed. Jerome Rosenberg, Dept. of English, Miami University, Akron, Ohio).